THE
GOOL
Sex
GUIDE

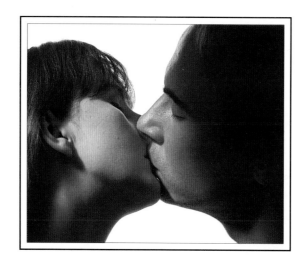

—THE—
GOOD
SEX
GUIDE

THE ILLUSTRATED GUIDE TO ENHANCE YOUR LOVE-MAKING

Dr David Delvin

EBURY PRESS · LONDON

THIS IS A CARLTON BOOK

FIRST PUBLISHED IN GREAT BRITAIN IN 1993
BY EBURY PRESS
AN IMPRINT OF RANDOM HOUSE UK LTD
RANDOM HOUSE, 20 VAUXHALL BRIDGE ROAD
LONDON SW1V 2SA

© CARLTON TELEVISION LIMITED,
CARLTON BOOKS LIMITED AND
PROSPECT PICTURES LIMITED 1993

This book accompanies the ITV series *The Good Sex Guide* made by
Prospect Pictures for Carlton Television

A catalogue record for this book is available
from the British Library

ISBN 0-09-177871-9 (hardback)
ISBN 0-09-177872-7 (paperback)

PHOTOGRAPHY BY KEN NIVEN
PROJECT ART DIRECTION BY RUSSELL PORTER
DESIGN BY TOWN GROUP CONSULTANCY
DESIGN © 1993 CARLTON BOOKS LIMITED

REPRODUCTION BY DOT GRADATIONS
PRINTED IN ITALY

CONTENTS

foreword by Margi Clarke

Sex is one of the most important things in life; in fact for me it tells me more than anything about the mystery of life. It's just such sheer pleasure; it's not taxed and you can enjoy it whether you're rich or poor, young or old, powerful or powerless.

It's the biggest gift we've been given. Relationships, I think, have been sent to us to show us how to be ourselves and to help us to grow. It's all on the menu from on high. No matter what our bodies look like, someone can love us for our true selves. Beauty is only on loan anyway, but in a long sexual relationship you can be given such marvellous confidence that no matter what you look like you're important and you count.

Passion in the first flush of love can wane, but good sex can last and get better. When I was younger I looked at my Mum and Dad and thought 'ugh... how can they touch each other let alone jump up and down together?' Now I'm older I really understand how long-term relationships blossom with the passage of time: you're not just making love to somebody's body, but to their soul. Apart from sex being of course safer when you're with one partner, it's also more fun as you embark on a continuing adventure of sexual exploration.

What I've discovered while making the television series *The Good Sex Guide* is that all that stuff about British reserve isn't true – behind those net curtains of suburbia lurk dildos, vibrators and love balls! In the charts at the end of the chapters in this book you can read some of the surprising things we discovered in our sex survey of the Great British Public.

I really hope this book helps you to have even more good sex. And remember, fellas, making love to a woman with the aim of pleasing the woman will also increase your pleasure, and vice versa.

Although sex for me is the biggest ecstasy there is, I could live without it – but they'd have to carry me kicking and screaming to the nunnery!

Margi Clarke

Women and their Sexual Responses

*i*magine a woman lying back on a bed, being tenderly stroked. With skilled caresses, her lover arouses her to greater and greater heights of passion. As her heart beats faster and faster, she breathes more wildly. Her vagina begins to pour out creamy love juices and her nipples become erect.

Gradually, a delicate pink flush spreads over her skin. It reaches her breasts, where the veins are suddenly more prominent. The breasts themselves have grown in size during the last few seconds — and the darkish pigmented area around each nipple is so engorged that it seems to be almost bursting with desire. Encouraged, the lover continues with more enthusiasm.

Now the woman's breathing becomes more urgent as the moment of climax approaches. Every muscle in her body tenses in preparation for the instant of release. Her throat opens wide, and she's powerless to prevent a wonderful, thrilling scream ripping out from deep, deep inside her.

This is what it's all been leading up to. This is the moment of orgasm.

Well, that's how a woman reaches a climax in theory and it's great when everything goes according to plan. However, the truth is that much of the time, this is not what happens.

Every woman in the world finds that sometimes sex is unsatisfactory — even though she may not admit it — and every man should be aware of this.

So what can be done to make sex better and more satisfying for a woman? As we'll see in the course of this book, it's vital that the couple should pay attention to matters such as romance, sensitivity and emotion. But other things need to be considered first.

The SEXUAL MAKE-UP of a WOMAN

You cannot drive a car without learning where the steering wheel and pedals are, and how to use them. In the same way, good, satisfying sex is very difficult to achieve unless you know something about 'the controls'. 'The controls' in this case are the sexually excitable parts of a woman's anatomy. Whether you're male or female, understanding basic female anatomy is essential if you are to enjoy good sex. Although this may seem obvious, these are the important 'female parts' with which every would-be good lover should be familiar.

her breasts

Breasts vary a great deal from woman to woman, and it's common for a woman to have one breast larger than the other. But no matter what size or shape a breast is, it still has the same erotic potential as any other. Stimulating a breast correctly nearly always gives its owner tremendous sexual sensations.

Breasts are mainly made of fatty tissue, through which little tubes called milk ducts run down towards the nipple. Breasts also contain supportive tissue, and if this becomes very slack, the breasts tend to droop. Good tips to prevent this from happening are:

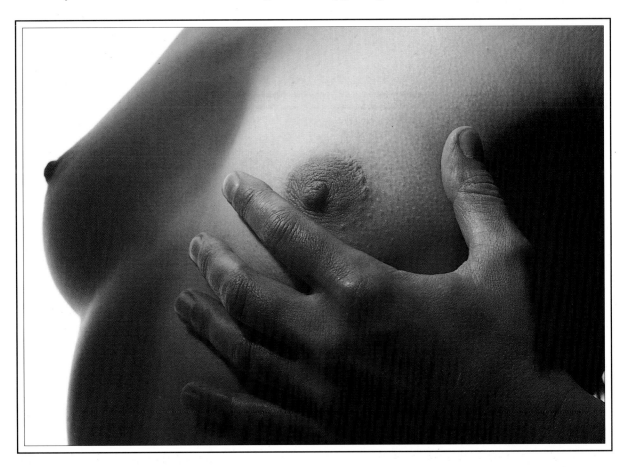

● Some women reach orgasm through nipple stimulation alone, but the majority of females cannot do this.

● The nipples have close nerve connections with the pleasure centres in the brain: they will respond powerfully to stimulus.

■ Don't become overweight.

■ Get plenty of exercise.

■ In particular, do 'pec-deck' exercises on a machine which is now available in most local gyms. These strengthen the pectoral muscles which support the breasts.

Although fashions change, people nearly always want breasts to be bigger. Almost everyone has a completely false impression of what normal breast size is – thanks largely to pictures of voluptuous pin-up girls with enormous bustlines. In fact, the average healthy woman has a bust measurement of just 34in (86cm). So it's nonsense to think that a large bosom is essential for a good sex life. Even the smallest breasts are little sexual timebombs. Give them a good caressing and the results will be explosive. Only rarely do women dislike having their breasts touched – usually after an emotional trauma, such as the loss of a baby.

her areola

The areola is the pigmented ring around the nipple. Surprisingly few people pay enough attention to the areola when making love. It's an extremely sexually sensitive area of a woman's body, packed with delicate erotic nerve endings. Simply running a well-moistened fingertip round the areola will pay rich dividends. In a minority of women, this technique can actually bring on a climax.

her nipples

The nipple usually projects forward — though a few women have inturned (inverted) nipples. Please note that if a nipple that normally projects forward

● In order to be a skilled lover, a man must learn how to stroke a woman's vulva in the way that most pleases her.

becomes inverted at any time you should immediately consult a doctor, as this can be an indication of cancer. The nipple is actually made of erectile tissue — in other words, tissue that becomes stiff and hard under the influence of sexual stimulation, as a man's penis does. Like the areola, it is positively bursting with sensual nerve-endings which are directly connected to the emotional areas of a woman's brain.

So, stimulating the female nipple (whether by hand, lip, tongue or vibrator) is an effective way to produce sexual arousal. Many couples find that the most arousing nipple-stimulation technique is for the man to take the nipple gently in his mouth and suck tenderly on it. But the emphasis is on the words 'gently' and 'tenderly'. If you are too rough with your mouth (or let your teeth catch your partner on her nipple), the effect may not be at all erotic. Having said that, some women enjoy the sensation when their nipples are lightly bitten, so it's worth finding out what your lover prefers.

her vulva

Many people don't understand the word 'vulva'. It just means the outside (or visible) part of the female sex organs. The word 'vagina' — discussed later on — means the interior part, which is not readily visible from outside.

A vital point for men to realize is that research has shown that many women feel extremely embarrassed about their vulvas and think they look ugly. So it's important for a good lover to be appreciative of his partner's vulva, and to reassure her that he finds it attractive and exciting.

her pubic hair

Pubic hair has always been considered outrageously sexy. Indeed, until quite recently, anyone who published a photograph of it would have been inviting a prosecution for obscenity, so it was routinely air-brushed out or covered up. The hair covers a good deal of the vulva, extends quite a bit above it, and varies in texture, depending on the woman's racial origin. However, in nearly all women it's fairly crisp and crinkly.

Though most people expect pubic hair to form a triangular shape, the fact is that this also varies a good deal from one woman to another. In particular, Mediterranean and Middle Eastern women may have pubic hair which extends quite a bit towards the navel, and sometimes onto the inner sides of the thighs. Many women are distressed about this and think that it is abnormal, even though it isn't.

Nevertheless, if you're not happy about the shape of your pubic hair, it's not a difficult matter these days to have it reshaped by the process known as 'depila-tion' (hair removal). You can go to a beauty salon to have this done, or use a depilatory cream yourself at home, taking care not to get the cream on any sensitive parts of your vulva. Alternatively, you can ask your partner to help you shave any unwanted hair. Many couples find it sexually stimulating to do this, particularly when they're enjoying a steamy session in the bathroom. And a number of people think that

it's very erotic for a woman to remove all her pubic hair (though be warned that, if you do this, it can be itchy as the hair grows back).

The roots of the pubic hairs are quite sensitive, so a good lover should remember that gently toying with the hairs, stroking them, or giving them little tugs, is an effective way of building up sexual tension.

her 'lips' (her labia)

The opening of a vagina is protected by two sets of lips (the medical name for them is 'the labia'). They are powerfully sensual parts of the body and stimulating them with the tongue or a finger is likely to give a woman very strong sexual sensations.

Many women mistakenly believe that their vaginal lips are 'ragged', 'too long' or 'not symmetrical' and find this very worrying. They often think that the lips have become distorted by masturbation, although this is quite impossible. In fact, the two pairs of lips (and particularly the outer ones) are designed to have rather bumpy-looking edges and be quite long as a protective measure, and there's no reason whatsoever why they should be symmetrical.

Drawing the skin gently upward over the pubic bone will increase the pleasurable tension in the labia.

her clitoris

Her clitoris is located just where the two inner lips meet at the front. To the touch, it feels a bit like a small garden pea. The clitoris is the equivalent of the male penis and is formed from the same type of tissue. This is why it stiffens and becomes erect when it is stimulated.

However, a clitoral erection is never massive. Some couples worry because the clitoris fails to stand up dramatically like a sort of mini-penis, but even when fully erect, the visible part of the clitoris isn't much bulkier than a medium-sized garden pea.

When a woman isn't in a state of sexual excitement, her clitoris is usually covered by a little fold of tissue called 'the hood'. But as she gets really turned on, her clitoris pushes itself outwards from under this hood and becomes more visible.

The way in which you should stimulate her clitoris is covered on pages 20–22.

her pubic bone

Though it's not (strictly speaking) part of the vulva, the pubic bone is well worth knowing about if you want to be a skilled lover.

For a start, it's a very useful reference point to help you find the famous G-spot (see page 25) discovered by Ernst Grafenberg. Secondly, during intercourse a good lover can try to compress his partner's clitoris between his own pubic bone and hers — thus greatly increasing the stimulation which he gives her. Thirdly, during various types of love play it's helpful to be able to compress the clitoris, and the upper parts of the vaginal lips, against the pubic bone.

So, it is a good idea to familiarize yourself with the pubic bone. You can easily locate it by running your fingertips straight down the mid-line of pubic hair until you encounter a hard ridge of bone just below the surface of the skin.

● Use a fingertip to discover her pubic bone; later on, it will help you to locate her G-spot.

her urinary opening

This is a tiny hole, a little way below the clitoris, and (like the clitoris) in the mid-line. Some people worry about it because they think it must be dirty since urine passes through it. In fact, it's not dirty at all, because urine is normally a completely germ-free fluid. So you can touch this opening without any risk of doing yourself any harm.

important note: Make sure that your fingers are clean whenever you touch this (or any other) part of the vulva or vagina. Dirty fingers could easily introduce infection.

Some women like to have the urinary opening stimulated, but on no account should anything be pushed into it. People sometimes do this in a spirit of experimentation, but it is a very bad idea, running the risk of infection or damage to the delicate tissues inside.

her vagina

The word 'vagina' means 'sheath' — and that's exactly what it is: a sheath which is the perfect size and shape to contain a man's penis.

When a woman is not sexually excited, her vagina is about 7.5cm (3in) long. This is obviously a lot less than the length of the average erect penis. But when she becomes really turned on, her vagina expands in the most extraordinary way, stretching out to a length of 17cm (about 6⅔in) or more in some cases.

There are two other facts to know about the vagina. First, although its walls are quite tough and resilient, there's a limit to the amount of pounding it can withstand. A lover should always treat his partner's vagina gently; if its owner says that what he is doing is hurting, he should stop doing it immediately.

Secondly, it's now known that when a woman is sexually excited the walls of the vagina produce love juices which lubricate intercourse and help to make things easy and pleasant. So, if you find that penetration is difficult because the vagina is still quite dry, this may be an indication that you should spend some more time on foreplay until the vaginal juices really start to flow. Some women are dry because they are menopausal, in which case some type of lubrication, such as K-Y Jelly, will help to make penetration easier.

typical sexual response
in a woman

When a woman has a really sexy session with her man, what happens? Well, in most instances the scenario will probably go something like this.

- In the early stages of the encounter, when they're fancying each other and enjoying a romantic, amusing or erotic conversation, the woman's pulse starts to speed up as more and more blood is pumped into her sexual organs.
- Once the foreplay becomes more physical and she gets more interested in the possibility of sex, her labia start opening up in preparation for receiving his penis.
- As she gets even more turned on, fluid begins to flow from her sex organs — not just the love juices from her vaginal walls, but also lubricating fluid from glands around the opening of her vagina.
- At the same time, her nipples start to lengthen. In an average woman, they will increase in length by up to a centimetre (half an inch) and their diameter will increase by a similar amount.
- The colour of the inner part of her vulva will change, usually shifting from pink to a red or deep wine shade.

All these are signs that she is getting ready for sex and that her body is beginning to prepare itself for the build-up to orgasm. During the next few minutes, all these changes will become more intense. Pulse, blood pressure and respiration rate will all

● Intense sexual stimulation leads a woman into the first of three stages of orgasm, when her mind often seems to pause to 'take stock' before she finally presses on to reach her climax.

increase, her eyes will become glazed and dreamy, and her mind will slowly lose interest in the boring realities of everyday life and begin to concentrate on the quest for a really enjoyable climax.

ORGASM — and FAKING ORGASM

Now what happens when a woman actually 'gets there'? Let's begin with the feelings in her mind. The great American sex gurus Dr William Masters and Virginia Johnson, authors of the bestselling Human Sexual Response (1966) and On Sex and Human Loving (1986), claim that from a psychological point of view there are three stages in female orgasm.

1 After being sexually stimulated for a while, the woman often has a curious sense of cessation or stoppage. It's as if her mind has paused to take stock for a second or two before pressing on towards the climax.

Almost at the same time, the woman is likely to experience an isolated thrust of intense sensual awareness. In most women, this intense feeling centres on the clitoris – but also radiates upwards into the innermost parts of the sex organs. The moment of climax will vary according to the nature of the stimulation.

Some women have a feeling that they want to expel something from inside them at this moment, and recent research has shown that many do indeed squirt out a small amount of special sex fluid at this time.

2 In the second stage of orgasm, say Masters and Johnson, women experience what's termed a 'a suffusion of warmth', which spreads through the whole of the pelvic area (that is, the lower part of the woman's body).

From the pelvic area, this warm, pleasant feeling spreads out into the tummy, chest, arms and legs.

3 In the third and final stage of orgasm, most women develop a wonderful sensation of pelvic throbbing. In other words, they feel a repeated series of contractions in and around their vaginas. Many report that this agreeable feeling is the most pleasurable of all human sensations.

While all this has been going on, many other things have been happening to her body. Some of them are mentioned at the very beginning of this chapter. Others which a lover may notice — so that he can tell with reasonable certainty whether or not she has climaxed — include the following:

■ Her face will usually go into a sort of a grimace, almost as though she is in pain.

■ The muscles of her arms and legs will usually go into a violent spasm.

■ Her toes will curl up — this is a very good indication that orgasm is occurring.

■ The muscles around the opening of her bottom will twitch spasmodically.

■ As the orgasm finishes, the nipples may stand out even more prominently than before. This is because the woman's breasts start to shrink a little as soon as orgasm has been achieved. This slight shrinkage can make the nipples appear to jut out more from the breast.

faking orgasm

The above are some of the ways in which a lover can detect whether his partner has come. However, in actual practice it's very easy for a woman to fake orgasm. If you've seen the film When Harry Met Sally, you'll have witnessed a good example. That was the movie in which Meg Ryan cheerfully simulated an orgasm in the middle of a crowded

● In the second stage of orgasm, women often feel a wonderful sensation of warmth suffusing the pelvic area.

restaurant (thus provoking a woman at a nearby table to tell the waiter: 'I'll have what she's having. . .'). Most women who have ever had an orgasm — or who have, perhaps, seen somebody else having one — would have no difficulty in putting on a display which would fool most men into thinking that they've climaxed. But the important question is should they do it?

The majority of doctors involved in sexual medicine will say that it's a bad idea to fake orgasm. This is because they have seen so many relationships where the woman has got into the habit of faking. The couple's sex life has deteriorated into something of a sham, with the man ejaculating and going to sleep, repeatedly leaving the woman unsatisfied.

On the other hand, there are some independent-minded women who say that it is justifiable to fake orgasm occasionally. They cite the following instances:

- At the start of a new relationship, if you realize that — perhaps because you haven't grown used to the man or his love-making technique — you aren't going to have an orgasm, even if you continue for hours.
- When you're very tired (too tired to orgasm, in fact), but you feel that your man will be happier if he thinks you've got there.
- When you're with a man who desperately needs his woman to come — or else he feels a failure.

Whether you should fake orgasm or not is a difficult moral issue. Ultimately, this must be a personal decision based on your feelings and the circumstances, but if you decide to fake orgasm, take care not to make a habit of it or your relationship may suffer because of your lack of sexual fulfilment. If it is difficult for you to achieve orgasm through penetration, and you almost feel obliged to fake an orgasm, it may be that you will find it easier to bring it on through masturbation (whether the stimulation is done by yourself or your partner). In this case you should try to accept the situation as a couple and adapt your love-making accordingly.

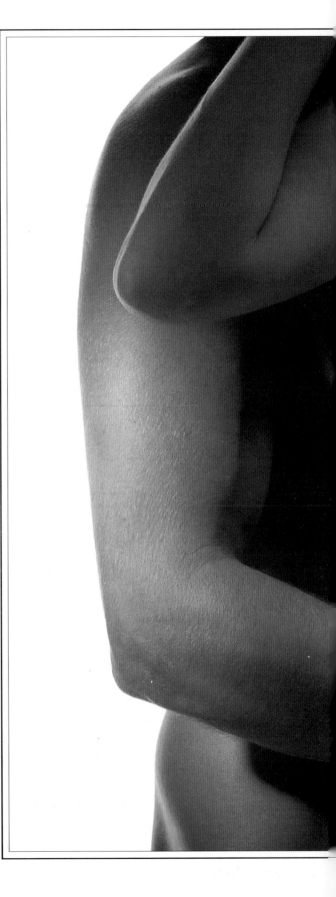

In the third stage of orgasm, many women feel an intense sensation of pelvic throbbing.

improving sexual response in a woman

How can a man make sex better for his lover? Well, the solution is not just to try out a new technique or buy the latest sex aid, although there's certainly a need for good techniques, and in many relationships there's also a place for good sex aids. But in every worthwhile relationship, a man has to provide certain other things too. They include:

- *Sensitivity* — in other words, being sensitive to a woman's needs, feelings, moods and desires. If you can't attune yourself to her emotions, you are never going to be very successful as her lover.
- *Romance* — old-fashioned as it may sound, nearly all women love romance. Survey after survey shows that this is one of the things they most want from a man. Sharing a candlelit dinner, giving her flowers, or playing a special song on a jukebox, for instance, are all romantic gestures that few women will be able to resist.
- *Praise* — which means praise of her body (particularly her breasts and sex organs), of her face, and of her ability to make love. Remember that many people — female and male — feel that their bodies and their sexual abilities are inadequate in some way. A word of affirmation and encouragement from a lover can make all the difference — and can stimulate a woman to heights of sexual enjoyment which she's never reached before.

In addition to all this, a man who wants to make his woman happy should familiarize himself with some of the technical aspects of satisfying her. In particular, he should learn about cunnilingus (see page 119) and indeed about other sex techniques she might enjoy. But most of all, he should learn about stimulating the clitoris.

the clitoris and the need to stimulate it

The basic anatomy of the clitoris, and the fact that it is the woman's equivalent of the penis, has already been mentioned. However, the essential thing for men to appreciate is that, in most women, the clitoris is the real key to their sexuality.

If you're a man, you need to say to yourself that, sexually speaking, a woman's clitoris is as important to her as your male organ is to you. In almost any sexual encounter with a member of the opposite sex, you should never forget to pay attention to that agreeable little button. Stroke it, caress it, lick it, suck it — in fact, do whatever she finds most pleasurable.

If you have any doubts about how vital it is to do this, bear in mind that the great majority of women simply cannot climax unless they have a good deal of clitoral stimulation. Admittedly, the clitoris gets some stimulation in many positions of sexual intercourse. But for good results, you really need to give it fairly intensive stimulation with love play, using your fingers or lips — or perhaps a vibrator.

DO MEN KNOW WHERE IT IS?

Most surveys suggest that many men are a bit vague about where the clitoris is and this is particularly true with inexperienced men. This is not so surprising since there are still quite a lot of women around (especially younger women) who don't know where their own clitorises are, unbelievable though this may seem! An easy way for them to find out is to ask for advice next time they have a cervical smear test done. The sympathetic women doctors at clinics are only too used to picking up a mirror in order to show a patient the location of her little love button.

Still, things are improving. A generation ago, it is probable that most men neither knew nor cared about the clitoris, and as a result, their partners were often very frustrated.

Improving sexual response in a woman requires sensitivity, romance — and praise of her attributes.

Whatever he does, a man should begin any attempt at clitoral stimulation gently. Start by caressing the area outside, gradually moving inwards and exploring with your fingertip or tongue. If the area is a little dry and you are using a finger, try licking it first to add some moisture. Once you've found the clitoris and hit the right spot, keep the pressure firm and fast, but take care not to be rough or to scratch her with a fingernail.

However, if you find it impossible to achieve success, the best thing is to ask the woman to show you what to do. She might do this by taking hold of your hand and guiding your finger into place or she might stimulate it herself while you watch. The key is to let her tell you and demonstrate what is good for her, and with practice you'll soon discover what she really likes.

other erogenous zones
including the G–spot

In addition to the clitoris, a woman has many erogenous zones or areas which she likes to have caressed. If you pay special attention to your lover's erogenous zones, this will help you to turn her on. Here are some of the more important ones, ranging from the top of the body down to the feet. Remember, though, that what one woman may find particularly exciting may not be so stimulating to another — or, indeed, may even be an irritant. With experience, and by talking to your lover, you will discover where she really likes to be touched.

● It's worth caressing a woman's many erogenous zones — including her buttocks.

Don't forget to kiss her navel and ribs — areas that rate highly among the erogenous zones.

behind her ears

Most women love to be stroked, tickled and caressed behind the ears. Some become aroused when they are gently kissed here and others love to have their ears licked and their lobes sucked. Ears may be so sensitive partly because they are slightly secret places, rarely touched by other people. In general, any such nook or cranny of the female body is likely to be an erogenous zone.

the back of her neck

The nape or back of her neck is a very sexually sensitive place. Make a point of running your lips up her spine to the point where her hair begins.

her armpits

These are also rather secret places so try kissing, nuzzling and licking these intimate spots. You'll probably find that the subtle feminine scents which are produced in this region of her body will be a real turn-on for you too.

her wrists

Don't forget to kiss or lightly stroke the inside of her wrist — again, a spot that is rarely touched by others. One well-known psychologist, Dr Robert Sharpe, says that a sure-fire way of directing a person's mind towards sex is to offer to take over from them while they're doing the washing-up. 'But what you do,' he states, 'is to draw their hand gently out of the water — and then plant a loving kiss on the inside of their damp wrist.'

her ribs

Ribs can frequently be quite erotic structures — especially when a woman is slim, so that they're fairly prominent. Try running your mouth along them, kissing as you go, or following the contour of a rib with the tip of your tongue or finger — you'll soon discover what your lover likes best.

● Why not follow in the footsteps of the famous and try giving her a 'toe job'?

her navel

The tummy button can be a surprisingly sexy part of the body, and a rare minority of women can climax simply through having it stimulated. Even if this doesn't happen, however, you may find that if you just stroke it, kiss it, or run your tongue around it, this will give your partner, warm, comforting feelings.

her buttocks

The buttocks are very sensitive areas of the female body, richly supplied with sensory nerve endings. Stroking, kissing, patting and squeezing them are likely to be well received. Many couples go in for much firmer patting — in fact, smacking hard enough to produce some pain. This may not be something that you or your partner enjoy but, since so many do find it stimulating, it's certainly worth considering — provided that you don't become over-enthusiastic and inflict unpleasant levels of pain.

the insides
of her thighs

These are sexy, ticklish spots which it is well worth kissing, stroking and licking. But because they're very much on the 'final approach' to the vagina, it's usually best to leave the thighs until very late in the exploration of the erogenous zones, rather than making a lunge for them right at the start.

the backs of her knees

There's a theory that the nerve supply of the backs of the knees is somehow connected to the nerve supply of the clitoris. However implausible this sounds, nibbling and nuzzling the backs of your loved one's knees is likely to prove popular with her.

the soles of her feet

Again, this is a 'not much visited' part of the female body. Like other rather private places, the soles of the feet are likely to give her pleasant vibrations if you stroke and kiss them. But if she's ticklish, don't overdo it.

her toes

Quite a lot of women are turned on by what is termed a 'toe job' — in other words, sucking or gently biting one of her toes in a playful way. A few women also find that having their ankles lightly stroked is highly erotic.

her G-spot

I've deliberately left the G-spot (named after its discoverer, Ernst Grafenberg) till last, because it's definitely not an erogenous zone that you should go for in the early stages of love-making. But once you've stimulated your partner's clitoris and vulva, then it's often worth while moving on to the G-spot region.

There's a lot of medical argument about what exactly the G-spot is, if it exists at all. But the important thing to grasp is this: there is no doubt that a very large number of women experience pleasant and rather unusual sensations when the area referred to as the G-spot is massaged by the tips of a man's fingers.

Few men know how to find the G-spot and often they discover it by chance. However, it is in fact about 5cm (2in) or so up the front wall of the vagina. The best way to find it is to slip a moistened finger gently inside, and run it slowly up the back of the pubic bone. When you've travelled up with almost half your finger, start pressing quite hard with your finger pad against the firmness of the pubic bone. You may have to move around a little bit until you strike the spot, but with a bit of luck your partner will suddenly say to you something along the lines of 'Mmm . . . that feels interesting'.

Continue rubbing there, by moving your finger backwards and forwards, and the results should be wonderful for her.

MASSAGING EROGENOUS ZONES

It's a really good idea to massage your partner's erogenous zones. One vital note before you start: don't rush things. Most men think that a massage should involve the genitals as soon as possible. But few women are like that, so don't be in a hurry to get to her vulva.

I strongly recommend that you use an oil when doing a massage. You can buy expensive scented massage lotions from sex shops, but these could possibly cause an allergic reaction, especially when applied to more intimate parts. So, in my view, it's better to buy baby oil, which is inexpensive and very unlikely to cause any skin problems.

Warm the oil between your hands before you start — it's decidedly chilly when it comes out of the bottle! Having cupped a little in your palms, then a good move is to start by rubbing it gently into her feet. Then, using your fingertips as sensuously as possible, gradually work up her calves to the back of her knees. My personal tip would be to go no higher up the legs at this stage, but to switch to the back of the neck, where you can spend a few minutes easing and soothing away any aches and knotted areas.

Next, work down over her shoulders and arms, trying to dig your fingertips gently into the muscles. Only then should you move to the rest of her body — perhaps starting on her ribs or shoulder blades.

Quite late in the game, you can smoothly shift to her breasts, and then work downwards over her belly to her inner thighs. By the time you've got this far she will probably be desperate for you to go further.

● A gentle and romantic massage is a great way to embark upon an extended and fulfilling love-making session.

pelvic exercises to improve a woman's sexual response

One subject which we investigated while making the Good Sex Guide TV series was whether exercises could help a woman's sexual satisfaction.

There's no doubt that one particular set of muscular exercises can and do help a number of women. They're called 'pelvic floor exercises', and they are now widely taught at ante-natal and post-natal classes, and at some yoga groups and women's sexuality workshops.

The name 'pelvic floor exercises' has nothing to do with being on a floor; you can do them while sitting, lying down, standing up or wherever you like. The pelvic floor, in fact, is the name of the powerful muscle which surrounds a woman's vagina.

Unfortunately, it tends to become a bit slack after childbirth (particularly repeated or difficult childbirth), with the result that love-making often becomes less satisfactory. Pelvic floor exercises will usually put this problem right.

However, these exercises are useful for any woman, whether or not she's ever had a baby, because they tone up the whole vaginal area, and make it fitter and stronger. They give the woman the ability to grasp her man's penis while it's inside her, and they make it possible for her to enjoy intercourse more. Some women who have practised the exercises over a long period say they get heightened pleasure from orgasms too. So the exercises are certainly worth a try.

Happily, they're very easy to do. First, you tone up the front part of your pelvic floor muscle. You do this by simply imagining that you're trying very, very hard to stop yourself from passing water. Feel that muscle tighten up at the front of your pelvis and hold the contraction for 10 seconds. Then relax for 10 seconds. Repeat 10 times — which will only take you between three and four minutes.

Second, you need to tone up the back part of your pelvic floor. The trick here is to pretend that you're trying desperately to stop yourself passing a bowel motion. So, tighten up your bottom — tight, tight, tight. Hold it for 10 seconds, then release. Relax for 10 seconds, and repeat 10 times.

You should do both sets of exercises twice a day — every single day. It will take about six months to achieve any significant improvement, but by that time you should be noticing that your sexual response is definitely perking up.

VAGINISMUS

This is a common sexual problem among women — doctors at Family Planning Clinics expect to see several new cases each week. Vaginismus is a disorder in which the person's vaginal muscles contract violently whenever any approach at all is made to her vagina. She doesn't intend this to happen — she simply can't help it.

This contraction makes intercourse difficult and painful — and often completely impossible. As a result, some women with vaginismus may remain virgin for years after they have married. (A few actually have 'virgin births' because the man's sex fluid has managed to get inside her, even though his penis hasn't.)

If you have vaginismus, you probably think that there is some obstruction in your vagina, or that it's too small. Indeed, it's regrettable that some women who suffer from vaginismus have been erroneously told by a doctor that they are 'small made'. The reason why doctors make this mistake is they have been fooled by the violent muscle contraction which occurs whenever they try to examine the patient.

Why does vaginismus happen? Well, in many cases it's a hang-up originating from early childhood. If a girl has been brought up to believe that her vagina is a dirty, secret place, or that she has to keep things (especially male things) out of it at all costs, it's scarcely surprising that she will grow up vaginismal.

A useful test for this type of vaginismus is Delvin's Tampax Test. Do you shudder at the very idea of a tampon going inside you, and regard insertion of one as truly terrifying? If so, then you probably have the condition.

'Secondary' vaginismus is slightly different. It occurs in women who have had a traumatic or painful episode involving the vagina — which could be anything from a rape to a really bad dose of thrush. Because of the memory of what has happened, these women also experience a violent and involuntary muscular contraction whenever intercourse is attempted.

TREATMENT Don't waste your time with operations to try to enlarge or stretch the vagina. These outdated and inefficient methods have now been replaced by a simple relaxation technique which is taught to the couple together at Family Planning Clinics and also at clinics specializing in sex therapy.

Learning to relax, under the tuition of a woman doctor or therapist, may take anything from a week to several years. But it usually works very well in the end.

'FRIGIDITY'

I put the word 'frigidity' in quote marks, because that's what people call it. But really, it's a very misleading term because it suggests that the woman is cold, and that her condition is somehow her fault — which it isn't.

Frigidity is used to describe the condition when there is a lack of sexual desire in women — either primary (which means you've never really been very keen on sex); or secondary (which means that you were keen once, but have now lost interest).

Primary frigidity is caused by the same factors which cause vaginismus (see above) — namely, a repressive childhood in which you've been brought up to believe that sex is dirty and disgusting, and most definitely not something that a woman could get any pleasure from. Primary frigidity is less common than it used to be.

Secondary frigidity, however, is very common.

Some of the main causes of frigidity are:

- Tiredness
- Overwork
- Depression
- Anxiety states
- Falling out of love with your partner
- Marital discord
- Recent childbirth
- A recent major illness
- Recent major surgery
- Use of illegal drugs
- Certain drugs prescribed by doctors
- Excessive alcohol use

TREATMENT It's important to realize that there is no easy remedy which will suddenly make a woman desperate for sex. A lot of people — especially husbands — assume that doctors can prescribe some magic hormone which will put everything right, but this just isn't possible. A few sex clinics do prescribe injections of male (not female) hormone in an attempt to pep up the woman's desire, but it's doubtful that this treatment is effective. Also, it tends to produce acne, a deep voice, and a tendency to moustaches.

In my view, it's far more sensible to go to a doctor or therapist who will try to help the two of you sort out why the woman is lacking in libido. Sometimes this is very quickly done — for instance, if she's in a perpetual state of anxiety about the fact that her parents are sleeping on the other side of a thin bedroom wall!

Other times, it may take several months to establish the cause — or causes (there's often more than one). But once the couple and the doctor or therapist have developed an understanding of exactly why the woman is lacking in desire, you can begin to do something about it together. In some cases, the couple may need to restructure their sexual attitudes completely, trying to get rid of old inhibitions and develop fresh and romantic ways of loving.

For full advice, I suggest you begin by going to a Family Planning Clinic or else a clinic run by Relate (formerly the National Marriage Guidance Council).

VIBRATORS

While researching for the Good Sex Guide TV series, we found evidence that vast numbers of women now enjoy using vibrators in bed. In most cases they don't use a vibrator every single time, but regard the device as a helpful aid to love-making sessions.

In addition, we found that doctors who are experienced in the treatment of sexual problems are now recommending vibrators as a useful device to help women reach orgasm, or simply get turned on.

It's clear then that the man who wants to be a good lover should know something about vibrators and their use. He shouldn't feel threatened by them, as some males do, but should be prepared to use a vibrator if his partner wants him to.

How are vibrators used? The simplest answer is in whatever way a woman wants. But, in general, vibrators are mainly used on the clitoris, and inside the vagina. Sometimes the man holds the device; sometimes the woman holds it; and sometimes they both hold it together. Just do whatever feels comfortable and right at the time.

Various types of vibrator are available these days; the following are just a few of the most popular ones:

Joni's butterfly

This is a little battery-powered device which a couple attach to a woman's loins (using straps that go round behind her buttocks). The idea is to fasten it over her clitoris, so that it will vibrate sensuously over that organ as she moves around.

the imitation phallus

Most vibrators are actually shaped in an imitation of a penis. They vary in size from the very small to the very large and can have textured surfaces. They can be gently eased inside the vagina, or just laid against the clitoris and left to buzz away. Nearly all these imitation phalluses are battery-powered and some can be quite noisy, which may prove off-putting to some women.

● Vibrators are now immensely popular. They can be used on the breasts as well as on the vaginal area.

the angel's egg

As the name suggests, an Angel's Egg is egg-shaped; it's a small device connected by a slim wire to a battery unit. The general idea is that you put it just outside the opening of your partner's vulva and let it lie there and throb.

the pistol grip

There are some vibrators which the man holds in his hand like a pistol or a power tool. When he pulls the trigger, a textured 'head' at the front of the device vibrates strongly against the woman's clitoris. Some of these vibrators run off mains electricity, and so they should never be used near water or they may cause a fatal accident.

There's a distinct tendency in men to like these pistol grip vibrators — doubtless because they enable them to act out cowboy fantasies in the bedroom! If you're a woman who doesn't mind 'Wild West' games, you could do worse than buy your personal sheriff a pistol grip for his birthday.

can men learn anything from gay women?

One of the questions investigated during the preparation of the TV series was whether male lovers can learn anything from the skills of gay women.

It emerged that doctors who are involved in sexual research have discovered that very often the caresses used by women who make love to other women are extremely gentle and skilled. This is scarcely surprising — after all, being women themselves they are more likely than a man to know exactly what turns a woman on and what is less likely to.

Few women making love to each other get into the sort of strap-on dildo techniques which men often fantasize about or imagine that they use. Instead, women tend to bring their partners to climax by the slow and sensitive use of fingers, tongues and lips around the nipples, vulva and clitoris. There is no doubt that a man who wants to be a skilled lover definitely has something to learn from this unhurried and tender approach to the female body.

Are you happy with the number of times you reach an orgasm or would you like to reach an orgasm more often?

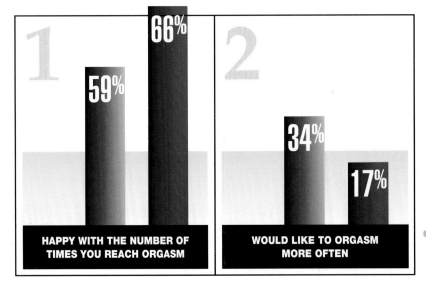

1 — 59% — 66%
HAPPY WITH THE NUMBER OF TIMES YOU REACH ORGASM

2 — 34% — 17%
WOULD LIKE TO ORGASM MORE OFTEN

— *women*

— *men*

● Over a third of women would like to orgasm more often: twice as many women as men.

Did you or have you ever faked an orgasm...?

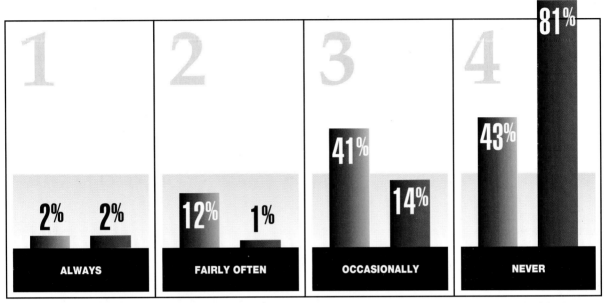

- 2% of both men and women appear always to pretend to have an orgasm. But 41% of women compared with 14% of men say they occasionally fake one. Only 43% of women (compared with 81% of men) say they never fake.

When making love do you have an orgasm/climax...?

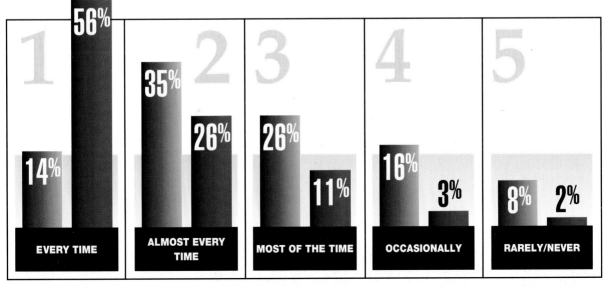

- Over 50% of men have an orgasm each time they make love, while only 14% of women do.

Men and their Sexual Responses

When a man comes, what actually happens? As a doctor, I find that many people (especially women) don't really understand what a male orgasm is.

The answer is this. A man's climax is nearly always caused by stimulation of his penis — that stimulation may be provided by his lover's vagina, her hand, or some other part of her body, or his hand, or a vibrator, or whatever.

Unlike women, men are not usually able to reach orgasm as a result of stimulation of another part of their body. From time to time, there are newspaper reports of men reaching orgasm through having their big toes sucked or their ear-lobes tickled, but most doctors view these stories with suspicion.

There is admittedly one obvious exception to the rule that male orgasm requires direct stimulation of the penis. This is that men — particularly when in their youth — frequently reach orgasm in their sleep while having erotic dreams (wet dreams). However, although it appears that in this instance the man is climaxing without any stimulation of his penis, in practice, it seems likely that friction of his pyjamas or the bedclothes on his organ may well play a part in making him come.

● At the moment of orgasm a man's face can look almost as if he is in pain rather than feeling intense pleasure.

It's important for women who want to be good lovers to realize that men do need direct stimulation of the penis in order to reach orgasm. This is simply because unless the man receives this kind of direct stimulation, he may have some difficulty in making it — especially if he's no longer young.

This does not mean that there are no other factors which help to bring about male orgasm. Psychological ones, for instance, are extremely important, and these and the emotional aspects of the male climax will be looked at later (see page 50). But the fact remains that if a man is going to reach an orgasm, he has to do it through friction applied to the sensitive nerve endings in his penis. This friction will help him go through the four stages of sexual arousal, which are as follows:

first stage: excitement

This stage of excitement is the one in which a man's sexual drive really starts to build up. His penis becomes very stiff, and his heart rate, breathing rate, and pulse rate all go up. Various natural chemicals begin to course round his bloodstream, preparing his body for orgasm.

second stage: plateau

The plateau stage is the one in which the man has achieved a high level of sexual tension, but is still in control of himself. Skilled lovers can maintain this plateau stage for half an hour or much longer if they want to, using it to enjoy sex with their partners before going over the top into orgasm.

Unfortunately, in many men (especially young men) the tendency is for the plateau stage to be extremely short — and they come far too soon. What to do about this problem is discussed on page 51.

third stage: orgasm itself

This is the stage of no return — when the man just has to let go (or rather come). Good lovers can take themselves up to the very brink of this stage again and again and retreat from it if they want to. But even the world's best-controlled man will sometimes go into this orgasmic stage before he means to.

There are several physical reactions during this stage. It begins with a fraction of a second in which the man's semen gushes into the lowest part of the tube that runs through his penis. American sexologists call this fraction of a second 'the moment of ejaculatory inevitability' because, after this, orgasm becomes completely and utterly unavoidable. There is now nothing in the world that the man (or his partner, or anybody else) can do to hold it back. You could point a gun at the his head, but it would not prevent the inevitable. He now has to reach orgasm.

The sudden gush of sex fluid, which comes from the prostate and nearby glands, spurts into the tube at the base of his penis, rapidly distending it to several times its normal width. The tube can't take that volume of fluid — and so it responds by pumping it out very quickly and very powerfully in a series of surges which send the liquid shooting out beyond the end of the penis. These surges are, of course, intensely pleasurable for the man.

In a particularly strong orgasm — and orgasms do vary in strength — the semen can sometimes shoot as much as a metre (over 3ft) away. But in most male climaxes, the thrust behind it is only powerful enough to drive the creamy liquid about 7.5cm (3in) or so. That's more than enough for reproductive purposes, since the whole reason for these spurts is to get the sex fluid into the top end of a woman's vagina — which is almost always very near the tip of the man's penis during intercourse.

How much fluid should the male produce at this climatic moment? The average is about a teaspoonful, or 5ml — a lot less than many people think.

When you consider all the effort involved, perhaps this does sound like a small amount, and indeed, many men are convinced that they produce far more than that (laboratory experiments invariably prove them wrong). However, the quantity produced does vary from day to day, and if you have repeated sex — say every few hours or so — you will probably reduce the volume a great deal. Conversely, if you don't have sex for several weeks or so, the volume which you produce when you next come will probably be a good deal greater than average.

Although the volume of seminal fluid is relatively small in all men, it's essential to remember that, unless you are sterile, there are going to be several hundred million tiny sperms in that teaspoonful of fluid. (Advice on how to avoid pregnancy and the importance of using condoms can be found on pages 138–9 and 104–6 respectively).

One curious statistic emerged while we were researching facts and figures for the Good Sex Guide TV series. Every night of the week, something like 20,000 litres (about 4,400 gallons) of this remarkable fluid is pumped into British women's vaginas during about 4 million orgasms!

fourth stage: **resolution**

This is the last of the four stages of orgasm. The term resolution phase (which was coined by the American experts Masters and Johnson) really means that this is the period in which everything calms down and returns to normal.

In this stage, most men start to lose their erections, though a few — mainly younger males — do not. Women should be aware that sometimes the penis may be very tender to the touch for a minute or two. The man's pulse rate, breathing rate and blood pressure now return to normal, and very often, special sedative chemicals are produced by his nervous system, damping down the activity of his brain and making him feel drowsy. This is why so many men fall asleep immediately after orgasm.

One final point about the 'resolution phase' is that scientists regard it as lasting until the man is capable of having an orgasm again. Women also have a resolution phase — but it is far shorter than it is in men. A couple should appreciate that while a women who has come may well be able to do so again very quickly, most men will not be able to.

In young men, the resolution phase may be over reasonably soon, and it is certainly not unusual for a male teenager to be able to climax twice within an hour. But as men get older, the resolution phase becomes longer and longer, so that an elderly man might well find that having had one orgasm, he is unable to climax again for another 24 hours or so.

To achieve a good or even better sex life, in the same way that you need to know about the sexual parts of a woman, whether you're a man or a woman, you really do need some knowledge of basic male anatomy.

The sexual structure of men is much simpler to understand than that of women — partly because most of the sexual equipment is on the outside, where you can see it without difficulty. Let's consider the parts one by one.

his penis

The most important thing for women to realize is that a man's penis is extremely precious to him. Most men think about (and worry about) their penises from a very early stage in life, right up until old age.

So what is this structure that they make such a fuss about? It's a fleshy organ, which in its non-erect (limp or flaccid) state is about 7.5–10cm (3–4in) long. More about length in a moment.

Inside, the penis is made up of three cavities — like three little cigars — which can fill up with blood during sexual excitement. It's this filling-up process (sometimes called 'tumescence') which makes the penis stiffen into erection.

Running in between the three cylinders, there's a little tube, smaller in diameter than a ball-point pen, which runs from the base of the penis to its tip — where it emerges. The little opening at this point

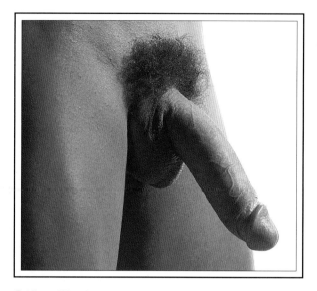

● Like a filling hosepipe, the penis then expands.

is about ⅓in (7mm) long. Seminal fluid and urine both pass through the tube. The fact that the penis is a urinary organ as well as a sex one is responsible for numerous sexual hang-ups and inhibitions — particularly as most children are brought up to regard urine as 'dirty'. As I mentioned in the previous chapter, urine is not in fact dirty at all; except in some rare instances, it's a sterile fluid (that is, it doesn't contain germs). It follows, then, that the penis is not, as many people think, a dirty organ. Its urinary tube doesn't normally contain any significant amounts of germs, and (unless you are suffering from some form of VD or other sexual infection) it can't transmit diseases.

What about the outside of the penis? Well, most of it is covered with soft skin, in which there are prominent veins. The vital thing to appreciate about this soft skin is that it's very sensitive and is packed with more sexual nerve endings than anywhere else in the male body.

If you're a woman, bear in mind that this organ, with its sensitive skin, is the equivalent of your clitoris: in other words, it's the sexual nerve centre. Whatever you do to that soft skin (within reason), from stroking it with your fingertips to touching it up with your tongue, will be very pleasant for your man and may indeed induce orgasm.

The tip of the penis is amazingly sensitive too. In shape and colour, it's rather like a plum, and its

● Mental or physical stimulation make blood enter the penis.

medical name is the 'glans'. Its surface, which has a pleasant velvety feel to it, is what nuzzles up against the top end of the vagina during intercourse.

Another important part of the penis is the foreskin. Also known as the prepuce, this is the part of the skin which covers the tip of the penis in babyhood. As a boy grows older, his organ gets bigger,

The internal pressure helps it toward full erection.

and the glans should emerge from the foreskin. However, especially in cold weather, quite a lot of the glans is usually hidden by the foreskin.

When a man gets an erection, the foreskin should roll right back, so that the glans is completely uncovered. Unfortunately, in a minority of men this does not happen; the foreskin won't go back, so that the glans remains covered — even during sexual intercourse.

This is an unhygienic state of affairs, as well as being unsatisfying sexually. If you're a man whose prepuce won't go back, you should have it removed surgically — an operation known as circumcision.

Circumcision is carried out routinely in Jewish male babies, and in older Muslim boys, but nowadays only a very small minority of boys are circumcized for medical reasons (usually because the foreskin is too tight to let them pass water easily). People argue endlessly about whether or not the circumcized penis is 'better for sex' than the uncircumcized one. In fact, there is no clear evidence either way. However, a circumcized penis is easier

to wash and keep clean, and cancer of the penis (fortunately a rare condition) is almost unknown in circumcized males. The danger with circumcision is that it can lead to unpleasant complications like excessive bleeding or infection.

his testicles

A man's testicles (his balls) are his two sex glands. They're located just beneath his penis, inside the little pouch of skin called the scrotum. They have two functions:

- To produce male sex hormones, which flow round the bloodstream and give the man his male sex characteristics, such as a beard, hairiness, muscularity, a deep voice, aggression, and desire for women.
- To produce the sperms which swim in the man's seminal fluid.

The average testicle weighs about 12gm which is slightly under half an ounce — less weighty than most people would think. It's roughly oval-shaped and is about 5cm (around 2in) in length and 2.5cm (about 1in) across.

It's quite common for one testicle to be slightly larger than the other; this is nothing at all to worry about. Also, one normally hangs lower than the other one. The great majority of men are born with two testicles, though occasionally a doctor examines a man and finds that he has three. Quite a few men have only one testicle in the scrotum; this is usually because the other one has got stuck inside a little channel which leads up into the groin. In such cases, it's usually best to have surgery as early as possible in order to bring the testicle down into the scrotum or else remove it altogether. (An undescended testicle is quite likely to become diseased if it is left where it is.) If a man has only one testicle, he will still be able to perform in bed and father children.

From the woman's point of view, there are two things to appreciate about the testicles:

- Men like having them handled. They find this sexually exciting — but no amount of stroking or fondling the testicles can by itself cause an orgasm.
- These two glands are very tender so do not squeeze them hard, or accidentally hit them with your knee or elbow.

worries about penis size

As has already been mentioned, when a penis is limp (not erect) its length is usually about 7.5–10cm (3–4in). However, what should it measure when it's erect?

This question is important to most males. There are very few men who haven't at some time taken a tape measure and surreptitiously measured themselves — and then worried about whether they're big enough or not. Indeed, some men go through life utterly convinced that their penises are too small. In the great majority of cases, however, they are totally wrong. These are the real facts about the size of the penis.

- Astonishingly, most penises are very much the same size when they are erect.
  A male whose limp organ is a little on the small side will as a rule achieve something like a 100 per cent increase in length during erection — while the man whose limp penis is pretty large will often achieve only a 70 per cent increase in length when he becomes erect.
- The great majority of men measure between 15cm (about 6in) and 18cm (around 7in) long when they are in a state of sexual excitement.
- The reason why so many men think they are small is this: when a man looks down at his own penis, he gets a foreshortened view of it — in other words, he's on the receiving end of an optical illusion that makes it seem shorter than it really is. In contrast, when he looks at other men in changing rooms or wherever, he's seeing

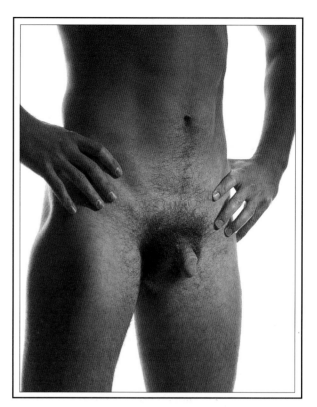

This penis looks somewhat small, but that is mainly because its owner is feeling cold.

This largish penis would probably be erroneously regarded by its owner as small.

This man's penis is on the large side when non-erect, but will be average size when he's excited.

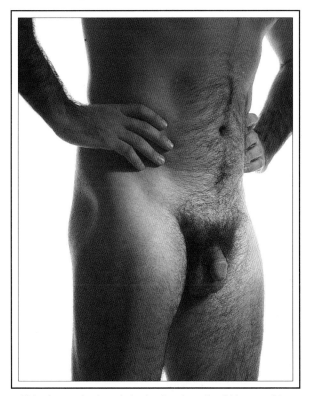

This circumcized penis looks tiny, but should be capable of lengthening to 15cm (6in) or more.

them sideways on — so their penises look longer.

■ If you want to get a more accurate impression of the length of your penis, look at yourself sideways on in a mirror. You'll probably be more pleased with the results.

■ Contrary to widespread belief, the penises of all races are very much the same length when erect. The myth that black men have bigger organs has been scientifically shown to be nonsense.

■ Size most definitely has no relationship to potency: a man can have a huge organ and be (a) not very virile; (b) a lousy lover.

Though these facts have been fairly widely known for some years, men continue to worry about whether they are big enough. This is quite unnecessary: as we've seen in the previous chapter, the vagina is a very elastic organ, so it will fit pretty snugly round almost any penis — no matter how big or how small it is.

For years, Agony Aunts and others have been trying to reassure worried men with the magic words 'size isn't important'. Despite this, some women who say that their lovers have large penises do tend to rate their sex lives slightly higher than those who say that their partners are on the small side. On the other hand, over 50 per cent of the women questioned in the survey for the Good Sex Guide TV series agreed that what a man does in bed is more important than the size of his penis. It's safe to assume that the majority of women would much prefer a skilled, kind, considerate, knowledgeable lover with a small penis to a man with a large one who is clumsy, selfish, thoughtless and ignorant.

One final point to bear in mind if you're one of the many males who feel inadequate where their size is concerned is this. Many women feel frightened or revolted by the idea of having a very big penis thrust into them; they regard it as threatening, and a potential cause of discomfort or even pain. So these women would much prefer you to be on the small side.

PENIS ENLARGERS

MEN AND SEXUAL AROUSAL

In preparing for the Good Sex Guide TV series we researched the subject of penis enlargers — sex aids which are claimed to make your organ bigger. We found that there's an extraordinary market for these devices, which are sold in large numbers through sex shops and by mail order. This is a testament to the remarkable enthusiasm which the human male feels for the idea that he needs a larger organ.

Most so-called penis-enlargers are plastic or glass cylinders, about the size of a half-bottle of wine. They have a rubber bulb connected to them via a tube. The theory is that you put the cylinder over your organ and then use the bulb to pump out most of the air, thus creating a partial vacuum. This vacuum 'sucks' your penis quite strongly, and may indeed give you an erection. It's rather like a woman giving you enthusiastic suction during oral sex.

The makers of these devices suggest that the suction process will make your penis get longer. 'Watch it grow and grow,' they say. Well, it's a nice idea, but in a lifetime of medical practice, I have seen no evidence that these things do any good at all.

So, why do so many men use them? Partly because they're desperate to be bigger, partly because they believe the well-written adverts for the cylinders — and partly because of the undeniable fact that the devices are quite effective masturbating machines. Indeed, one authoritative textbook on sex aids actually tells its readers that 'a developer can . . . help you masturbate while leaving hands free to hold a book or magazine, or fondle other parts of your body'.

Recently, battery-powered or mains-powered suction cylinders have appeared on the market. They work on exactly the same sucking principle as the simpler devices described above. Again, I have been able to find no evidence that they cause any increase in penile size.

Note: It has been claimed that excessive suction could cause bleeding or bruising in the penis, so if you do decide to try one of these devices, it is wise to use it only in moderation.

Women in pursuit of good sex should obviously know what usually turns men on and how to help this happen. We've seen earlier in the chapter that when a man begins to get sexually aroused, the first reaction is that his penis starts to become erect. This phenomenon is the equivalent of the lubrication which starts to occur in a woman's vagina when her mind turns to thoughts of intercourse.

But why does his penis get hard and stiff? Well, as I said above, the bulk of a man's penis is made up of three little cylinders. When he starts thinking about sex, quite a lot of blood begins to flow into these cylinders. Equally important, the tubes which would normally carry blood out of these cylinders begin to close. The result is that blood is trapped — under considerable tension — inside the man's penis.

The effect is very similar to what would happen if you blew firmly into a long balloon or a condom — it would stand out strong and proud. And that's exactly what a penis does when it becomes erect.

You may wonder why these mysterious alterations in blood flow occur. Initially, they're sparked off by changes occurring in the emotional centres of the man's brain when he starts to think about making love — and especially if his partner starts talking to him about sex. These changes send nerve impulses down his spinal cord to the 'sex nerves' in his pelvis, which supply his penis.

However, there's very often another, more 'local' factor: if you have been rubbing, stroking or sucking his penis, this sets off a reflex reaction involving his spinal cord which will help to alter the blood flow in his penis and so give him an erection. Incidentally, sucking is probably the most effective way of doing this. Countless men with erection difficulties have been helped by women who know how to suck a man into an erection.

The precise technical mechanism which alters the blood flow in the penis (so causing a hard-on) is still not completely understood by doctors, but recent discoveries suggest that it's all due to a hitherto unknown part of the nervous system. In 1992, medical

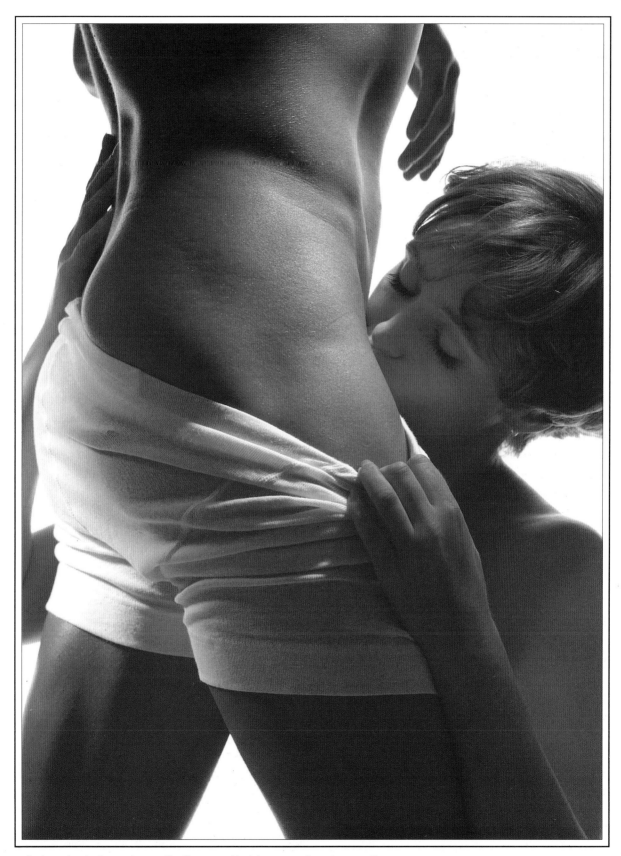

Oral sex is a loving and very effective way of helping a man to get an erection.

researchers reported that they may at last have unlocked the secret of male erection. Writing in the highly regarded journal Science, they claimed that they had found nerve endings in the penis which release nitric oxide gas during sexual stimulation. The researchers say that it is this gas which causes the changes in blood flow that lead to male erection.

Be that as it may, the important thing for women who want to be good lovers to remember is this. Helping a man to get and keep an erection is usually quite easy if you do the following.

- Stroke, fondle and rub his penis with your fingers.
- Suck his penis — often the most effective erection-inducer of all.
- Say sexy things to him — erotic words in his ear can be a powerful stimulant to erection.

MEN CAN'T FAKE ERECTIONS

While researching for the TV series with which this book is linked, we discovered that quite a few men wish they could fake an erection. These days there's considerable pressure on men to produce an erection at the drop of a hat, and very often they just can't oblige. One male patient told me: 'It's all right for women. They can fake being interested, but we can't.' Of course, this is quite true. A woman can pretend that she is interested in sex and go through with the sex act without too much difficulty. Her lack of arousal may mean that she doesn't produce any lubrication — but plenty of women fake this too, by discreetly applying one of the vaginal lubricants which are available from chemists.

It's impossible for a man to fake an erection, though a few men can, and do, fake orgasm occasionally — particularly when they're tired. How - ever, they don't do this with the same frequency as women.

● Though the penis is the most important, don't neglect your lover's other erogenous zones.

The UNRULY PENIS SYNDROME

Just as men can't fake their erections, they can't control them either and some women find this quite hard to understand.

Particularly when a man is young, his penis can decide to 'rise' at the most inconvenient times, often for no obvious reason. He may not be consciously thinking about sex at the time. This is a great source of embarrassment to many males — especially teenage boys — who may suddenly find that they develop an enormous bulge in their trousers while in a public situation.

These spontaneous erections can actually be very uncomfortable for a boy or a man, particularly if the penis gets caught in his underwear as it throbs its way determinedly to an unwanted erection.

There is no medical way of curing the Unruly Penis Syndrome. The only options when dealing with a spontaneous erection are to wait until it goes down of its own accord, to have sex (which may not be practicable), or to take the opportunity to masturbate in private. Some men, however, find that thinking unsexy thoughts can get rid of an erection quickly — perhaps imagining they are being chased by a gorilla or reflecting on a tricky problem at work, for instance.

EROGENOUS ZONES IN MEN

Most women will appreciate that by far the most important erogenous zone for a man is his penis. While sex does not have to centre on a woman's clitoris for her to be satisfied, it is not an overstatement to say that all sexually active men are obsessed with their own penises.

And yet, there are plenty of other erogenous zones in the male body and couples who neglect these areas in their love-making are really missing out. Here's a brief resumé, from head to foot. Remember that an imaginative woman can use her breasts as well as her hands, tongue and lips, to caress and arouse her lover.

Don't forget that your lover will almost certainly appreciate it if you lick and suck his earlobes.

his hair

Most men like having their hair ruffled and stroked, but this obviously does not apply if your man wears a wig or toupee. Bald men often like having the top of the scalp stroked and kissed.

under his jaw

There is a quite sexually sensitive area under the jaw, just on either side of the Adam's apple. Nuzzling and kissing here usually produces good results.

his ears

Most men's ears are just as sensitive as women's — in fact, this is one of the erogenous zones that the sexes share. Kissing, licking and nuzzling a man's ears are likely to turn him on, though some men hate it and find it too ticklish.

his back muscles

Nearly all men love having their back muscles stroked, massaged and gently prodded — especially after a hard day's work.

his nipples

Few people realize that, like the corresponding area in women, the male nipple and surrounding areola are sensitive. Stroking, kissing, gently pinching or nipping can often turn on a man.

his bottom

The buttocks and the anus are heavily supplied with sensual nerve endings. However, if you decide to stroke your lover around the anal area, make sure you wash your hands before touching anything else or you may risk infection.

his feet

Feet are quite sexy parts of the body, and there's now more public awareness of this following reports about women who are alleged to give 'superb toe jobs'. A 'toe job' simply means taking your man's big toe or any other one you fancy in your mouth, and making agreeable up-and-down sucking movements. Obviously, don't do it unless your partner is a hygienically-minded chap who keeps his feet clean and is free from fungal infections like athlete's foot.

MASSAGING EROGENOUS ZONES

Men really love having their erogenous zones massaged by women. That's one reason why massage parlours — especially topless ones — are so popular. So, if you feel like it, you should do your massage topless, and remember that — men being what they are — he will probably want you to finish the procedure by massaging his penis.

To begin, I suggest that you get your man to lie naked and face down on the bed. Lubricate your hands

Why not pour a few drops of champagne over his big toe — and then enjoy sucking it!

● Sitting astride him, use your outspread fingers to massage his bottom — a very sensual area of his body.

with a little baby oil or, if you haven't got any, an alternative is talcum powder, which makes the palms and fingertips slide over the skin.

Start by kneading his shoulders and upper back — many men have great tension here, especially if they've been working intensively. Curiously enough, if you dig your fingertips into places where he says it hurts, that will usually ease any pain and relax him.

I suggest you now work slowly down his spine, prodding gently in between the bones. When you get to his bottom, use your outspread hands to stroke his buttocks lovingly. Remember too that many men have a considerable enthusiasm for a few gentle smacks in this area.

Next, work up and down the insides of his thighs, and the back of his calves. Only then should you turn him over. By now, he may well be wild for sexual action (as you'll be able to see all too clearly). But you can prolong the fun a little longer, if you wish, by stroking his nipples and massaging the muscles of his belly before finally moving down to his by now eager sex organs.

WHAT MEN WISH WOMEN KNEW

A regularly recurring comment when people talk about their sex lives is: 'I do wish the opposite sex knew more about the way we feel and what we like when making love.' Both women and men make similar remarks.

Ideally, you should ask your partner what he/she wants in bed but many people find it difficult to do this or to respond. However, if you can overcome this communication problem, it really will pay dividends for your relationship.

If you're a woman, here are 10 suggestions to help you — these are some of the things that most men relish in bed:

1 *rude talk*
While there are a few men who insist on making love in perfect silence, most of them find it really

It is helpful to ask your partner what he or she most wants in bed — but do experiment as well.

exciting when a woman decides to 'talk dirty'.

2 appreciation

In the same way that women like to be flattered, men really love being appreciated in bed. Men cannot resist being told that they're in great shape, that they're good lovers, and — above all — that their penises are the best.

3 enthusiasm for sex

Some women and men still approach love-making in a half-hearted fashion, perhaps with one eye on the clock or on the TV. If you are enthusiastic about sex, he should react to match your mood.

4 laughter

Keeping a sense of humour where sex is concerned can be more valuable than a hundred orgasms. If you can give your man a bit of a giggle between the sheets, you'll be doing yourselves a lot of good. Some couples find that if sex is always a serious matter, stress can creep in, with adverse affects on performance and the relationship.

5 squeaking and screaming

Most men like their lover to make a bit of noise in bed — they think this shows what good performers they are. This may not be appropriate if there are children, parents or friends within earshot, but don't restrain yourself when you are in a position to shriek without embarrassment to you or others. If at all possible give a good loud indication of the moment of your climax so your lover knows that you've come.

6 willingness to experiment

In general, men tend to be more innovative than women when making love, and they often feel puzzled if a woman shows reluctance to try something new. Provided you feel you can cope with whatever your lover suggests it's often pleasantly exciting to vary your love-making technique, so keep an open mind and respond according to your feelings and the circumstances.

- Don't be afraid to let yourself go and scream while you are engaged in passionate love-making.

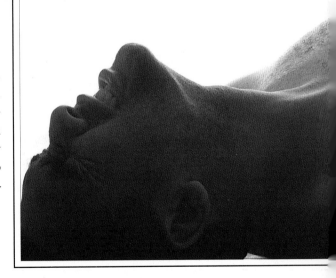

7 *willingness to try new positions*

Different sex positions can make love-making less routine. Remember that your man is likely to appreciate it if occasionally you take him by the hand and say 'Darling, I want you to have me in a completely new way...' Alternatively, let him find out by your actions what you have in mind!

8 *handling and massage*

As mentioned above, men invariably love being touched by women — most especially around their personal parts. A good tip is to keep a bottle of baby oil handy so that you can rub it lingeringly into all the more secret bits of his body whenever the mood dictates.

9 *dressing for sex*

A woman is more likely to want sex when she's feeling good about her appearance and is happy with what she's wearing. If she thinks she is looking unattractive she will in all likelihood feel unattractive too, and so may be unresponsive to sexual overtures. You probably won't feel sexy and confident of being desirable in underwear that should have been thrown away long ago and it is certainly unlikely to heighten your lover's desire for you. Similarly, he probably won't be turned on if he finds you covered with face cream. When you're dressing, or undressing for your partner, remember that some people enjoy making love while semi-nude, though most people agree that leaving socks on is undesirable.

10 *being willing to strip*

A number of women are reluctant to undress in front of their lovers because they think their bodies are less than perfect. However, most men find it very stimulating to watch a woman gradually take off her clothes and may feel disappointed if they are deprived of the opportunity to see her undress because she feels she is slighty over-weight or has breasts that are smaller than average. Stripping can be embarrassing for both partners, particularly in the early stages of the relationship, but remember that this can be an exciting part of foreplay.

The PSYCHOLOGY of MALE ORGASM

No woman has ever experienced a male orgasm and vice versa. So it's naturally difficult for one sex to understand exactly what the other sex feels at the moment of 'the big O'. However, it is particularly important for the woman who wants to be a skilled lover to try to grasp what happens in a man's mind when he comes.

The Reproductive Biology Research Foundation of St Louis, Missouri, has studied the psychology of orgasm in over 400 men aged 18 to 89. The Foundation reports that from a mental point of view, the male orgasm can be divided into two different stages:

stage one

This first stage begins with a moment described earlier in this chapter when the man realizes that he's going to reach orgasm very, very soon — and that there's nothing at all he can do to stop it, even if his partner begs him to delay for a while longer. Then there is an interval of two to three seconds during which nothing very much happens in his mind, except what the researchers describe as 'subjective experience of utter inevitability'.

stage two

At the beginning the man becomes aware of waves of enormously pleasurable sensations sweeping upwards from the region of the base of his penis. These are believed to be very like the pleasurable 'surges' which women experience during orgasm. The power of these waves of pleasure is so overwhelming that the man simply cannot think about anything else for a moment — although he may be vaguely aware of his lover's reactions, especially if she is urging him on.

In the latter phase of Stage Two, the man's mind usually concentrates on the fact that he is expelling what seems to him like a considerable volume of sex fluid, and which is immensely satisfying to his psyche. If he is actually making love at the time, he will probably do his best to thrust forward as far as

Willingness to experiment with different positions can bring fresh and exciting spice to a relationship.

possible — thus sending his 'love juice' as deep into his lover's body as he is able to.

From this research, it emerges that a man has surprisingly little mental control over his own orgasm. Once he starts to go, he cannot stop. This leads on to a subject that we researched in detail for the Good Sex Guide TV series as it is a source of anxiety for many men.

COMING TOO SOON

In many relationships (particularly those involving young couples) the man tends to be what can be best described as explosively triggered. In other words, he 'goes off' just a little too soon. In extreme cases, this is referred to as 'premature ejaculation' (see opposite).

Happily, there are certain things that a couple can do in order to make the man capable of lasting longer and postponing his orgasm. They include the following techniques:

- Make a pact that the man will tell the woman by some signal when he thinks orgasm is near.
- From that moment, she should immediately desist from wriggling, thrusting and saying or doing sexy things until he's managed to calm down.
- When he feels orgasm getting quite near, the man should employ what psychologists call 'distraction techniques'. This means that he should divert his mind from sex by thinking about something un-sexy — for example politics, football or work. (Which subject is un-sexy will of course vary from one man to another!)
- Additionally, he may be able to distract himself physically by clenching his teeth together hard, or by pinching or even biting himself!
- Changing the rhythm you might be moving to or simply pausing for a while may also help.

overcoming premature ejaculation

No one can say at exactly what point 'coming a bit too soon' becomes full-blown premature ejaculation, but the borderline isn't really relevant. Clearly, if a man climaxes so rapidly that he can't even get inside his partner, he has severe PE. Some people would say that a man who can't prolong intercourse beyond five minutes has mild PE.

From a practical point of view, if the simple measures outlined above haven't helped you delay the male climax very much, then it's probably time to seek professional help. Fortunately, an excellent self-help treatment for this kind of problem has been available for some years. Masters and Johnson achieved a 98 per cent success rate with it.

The most important part of this sex therapy is learning how to use a special grip which a therapist

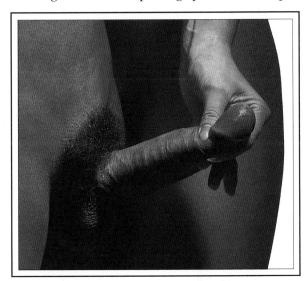

● The grip which cures 'PE' must be taught precisely by an expert; if it's wrong it won't work!

should teach the couple. When the woman applies this grip (which doesn't hurt) to the penis, it will immediately take away the desire to ejaculate.

There is rather more to the treatment than the simple outline I've given here. Often, the therapist has to help the two people reassess their attitudes to each other, and towards sex. In many cases, this process takes several months of counselling.

In Britain, this type of therapy is available from many Family Planning Clinics and from certain Relate centres, as well as from some doctors and psychologists in private practice. It is difficult, though not impossible, to obtain through NHS hospitals.

delay sprays

Another remedy sometimes tried in cases of premature ejaculation involves putting a local anaesthetic cream, ointment or spray onto the man's penis in order to try to reduce sensation during sexual intercourse. Such local anaesthetic preparations can be bought fairly cheaply at sex shops, and by mail order. They are not available on the NHS.

They sound fine in theory, but in my view they're only likely to help the most mild cases of pre-

mature ejaculation. They also carry the following two drawbacks:

■ Unless he is using a condom, a man who puts local anaesthetic on his penis will inevitably give his partner a dose of the local anaesthetic too, and this may interfere with her feelings and sensations, so depriving her of pleasure.
■ Most importantly, most local anaesthetics quite frequently cause people fairly violent and painful sensitivity reactions in their skin and delicate tissues. This probably wouldn't happen the first time of use, but might occur any time thereafter. To have one of these unpleasant reactions on your penis or in your vagina could be extremely nasty. For this reason, I personally do not recommend any of these preparations for treatment of premature ejaculation.

Have you ever worried about any of the following?

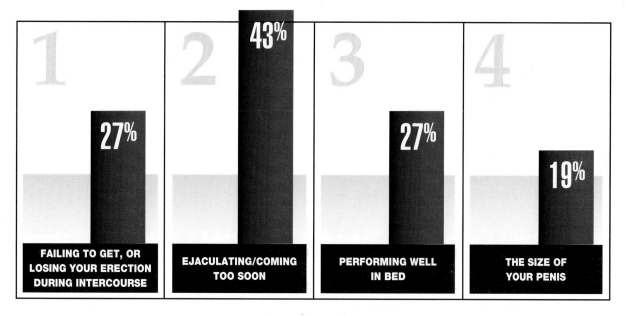

● Nearly a third of men have worried about failing to get or losing an erection. Over 40% have worried about premature ejaculation or coming too soon.

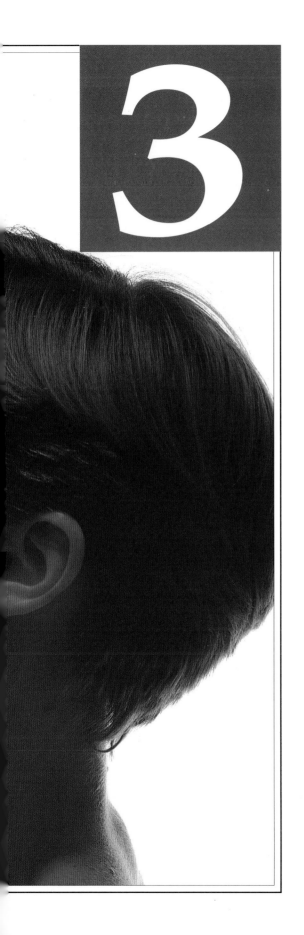

3

Sexual Inhibitions and How to Get Over Them

a good many people interviewed during the research for the Good Sex Guide TV series admitted to having sexual inhibitions. This isn't really surprising because, in fact, everyone has inhibitions of some kind. Psychologists will tell you that human beings comprise a mass of various inhibitions — some are sexual, but many are not.

For instance, nearly all of us grow up with considerable inhibitions or fear about getting ourselves burned through going too near a fire. We've developed that particular inhibition for two main reasons:

■ Way back in early childhood, our parents or elders 'inhibited' us from getting too close to the flames by pulling us away or telling us very firmly that messing around with fire was dangerous.

■ Second, if we were unwise enough to go near a fire, despite what we'd been told, we rapidly discovered that what we had been warned against was true — we did indeed get burned. This provided us with another powerful inhibition against playing with fire.

Now let's turn to sexual inhibitions. Virtually everybody in Western society is still brought up by their parents to regard their sex organs as being taboo. Even in the most liberated of households, there is parental pressure on children to hide their sex organs from strangers, and not to flaunt them in public.

In less liberal-minded homes, the inhibitions which parents instil are very much greater. Even today, it is quite common for very young children to be shouted at or even slapped by their mothers and fathers if they touch their private parts. If a parent screams at a child (or threatens her with violence) because she has been touching herself, it becomes a frightening signal which will imprint itself on her mind for life. For as long as she lives, she will retain something of that feeling that sex must be pretty dreadful — because if you touch yourself, you get hit or shouted at.

It's true that most Western families don't give children quite such a repressive upbringing as this today. But anyone who has worked with young children will tell you that a high proportion of them have been taught at an early age that the lower parts of the human body are rude. It is sometimes almost impossible for a doctor to examine a toddler with tummy-ache because his parents have drummed into his mind the idea that the lower part of his abdomen is 'dirty'.

These childhood restraints constitute a powerful reason for sexual inhibitions.

The human sex organs are arranged so that they're all mixed up with the organs of excretion. It is a great pity that people make love with the parts that they urinate with, for this has given vast numbers of men and women the most terrible hang-ups.

The odd thing is that — as mentioned earlier — urine is not actually a dirty fluid. People who are not doctors or microbiologists usually find this hard to believe, but it's absolutely true. Urine may not be the pleasantest liquid in the world, but it is normally germ-free. That's why people who have the curious habit of sipping their own urine — like some Indian gurus — don't actually do themselves any harm.

So, it's quite irrational that so many people have grown up with terrible sexual inhibitions based on the erroneous notion that urine 'makes the sex organs dirty'. On the other hand, it is quite true that people's bottoms (that is, their rectums) are dirty, because bowel motions contain large amounts of germs. These germs are not always harmful, but many of them can be dangerous to health. So it's quite right that children should be brought up to regard the back passage as a potentially contaminated area of the body — and be asked to wash their hands after touching it. However, parents shouldn't scream and shout at youngsters if they absent-mindedly scratch their bums or forget to wash their hands after sitting on the toilet. This kind of irrational parental disapproval is extremely likely to create hang-ups about the lower part of the body.

some inhibitions are good; some are bad

Some non-sexual inhibitions are good: for instance, the inhibition about sticking your fingers in fire. The same is true of some sexual inhibitions. You may find this hard to accept, but just consider for a moment what would happen if we had no sexual inhibitions at all.

Sex is, of course, a very powerful driving force in most people, and the sex act itself is usually extremely pleasant. So, if we had no inhibitions whatever then it is likely that we would all be having intercourse in the streets, morning, noon and night, with any reasonably personable stranger who happened along.

A tiny minority of people might think to themselves 'What a good idea . . . ' but, in reality, it would be a catastrophic situation. Marriage would break down totally, many women would be continuously pregnant without knowing who the father was, and AIDS (see pages 107–8) and other sexually transmitted diseases would spread like wildfire. In the animal world, there are plenty of species which have no inhibitions about sex, and where any male can have any female who happens to be on

You need to cast off your inhibitions if you want to enjoy your relationship to the full.

heat. But as humans, we actually need some inhibitions to keep us on the straight and narrow, although it's a pity that we've collected quite so many sexual inhibitions over the centuries, because they can simply clutter up people's love lives and make them deeply unhappy.

ALCOHOL and INHIBITIONS

Millions of people all over the world use alcohol to overcome their inhibitions — sexual and otherwise. The reason why alcohol works so effectively is that our inhibitions are controlled mainly by the front part of our brains. This front portion of the brain is cautious, careful and calculating — and it stops us behaving irresponsibly and irrationally.

What alcohol does is to damp down this front part of the brain, so that we become less cautious, careful and calculating — and less inhibited. That's why small doses of alcohol are very good for loosening people up and getting them chatting, when otherwise they might have been over-reserved or unforthcoming.

Small doses of alcohol can also aid your sex life a little — but only small doses. One or two modest-sized drinks can help you throw away your more constricting inhibitions, so that you have a wild time in bed with your partner.

On the other hand, larger doses of alcohol can have a really devastating effect on people's sexual inhibitions. Under the influence of alcohol, previously respectable people can do crazy things — like seduce their best friend's partner or have a passionate holiday romance with a total stranger. Excessive alcohol can also have a damaging effect on some men, who find that they become impotent — that is, they fail to get an erection and are afflicted with the aptly-named 'brewer's droop'.

Young people are especially vulnerable to the inhibition-lifting effect of alcohol, particularly if they're not used to it. In my capacity as an Agony Uncle, I regularly get letters from girls of 17 or 18 who have had a lot of drink poured into them by men who want to seduce them — and who have

ended the evening by having sex while so drunk that they didn't use a condom or any form of contraception. Consequently, they are extremely worried that they might be HIV positive (see page 107–8) or pregnant.

Other DRUGS and your INHIBITIONS

Because it is legal, sociably acceptable and easily obtainable, alcohol is the drug that is in the most common use. However, there are plenty of other drugs which people take in order to reduce their sexual inhibitions.

A number of the illegal substances that are widely used these days are popular mainly because they help to get rid of inhibitions and — in some cases — they increase the chance of sexual 'scoring' as a consequence..

In particular, Ecstasy (or 'E'), which has been used by tens of thousands of young people in the last few years, has a very powerful effect on damping down inhibitions. That's why in the UK (though not so much in the USA) it's employed as a 'dance drug' which makes people leap around happily all night. At the same time as reducing their sexual inhibitions, Ecstasy makes people feel very warm, tactile and responsive towards the people round them.

This may sound very pleasant, but the trouble with virtually every drug — including both Ecstasy and alcohol — is that before long, you start to need bigger doses in order to get the same liberating effect. Furthermore, every drug which reduces the inhibitions can have very serious side-effects. If you're tempted to make a habit of using heroin, cocaine or any similar drug to blot out your sexual inhibitions or for whatever reason, can I just remind you that — apart from being illegal in most countries — drug abuse carries serious health risks and inevitably creates more problems. In the following pages you'll find suggested some better and less damaging ways to overcome sexual and social inhibitions — and they don't carry the risk of an appearance in court.

inhibitions about meeting potential partners

Agony Aunties are inundated with letters from men and women who are desperately shy and anxious about meeting potential sex partners. Because of their inhibitions, many of them have no hope at all of ever going out with anyone — let alone forming a sexual relationship, getting married, or having children — unless, of course, they do something about it.

Why do they have these inhibitions? It's difficult to say, but many of them come from homes in which sex was considered a forbidden subject, in which sexual attraction between man and woman was regarded as 'not nice' and — very importantly — in which, as children, they were frequently put down by overbearing adults.

CASE HISTORY

Laura, a timid woman in her early twenties, wrote to my wife, who is an Agony Aunt on a TV programme. Laura said that she had never been able to look a man in the eye, and that conversation with a male was absolute torment for her. Typically, she'd been brought up by a strict mother, who'd given her the impression that all men were dangerous, and that sex was something frightful and to be feared.

Despite all this, Laura really wanted romance and love — and sex. But she was so inhibited that she couldn't even take the first faltering step along the road.

The remedy. **My wife put Laura in touch with an organization which provides assertiveness-training for women — mainly by taking them through role-play situations, group work and participation. She also recommended her to obtain the excellent 'anti-shyness' audio-cassettes which**

● Both men and women can be affected by inhibitions which detract from their enjoyment of their love lives.

have been developed by the well-known psychologist Dr Robert Sharpe and can be bought by mail order.

Two months later, Laura was able not only to look a man in the eye, but to ask him out on a date. Later that year, she had a couple of fairly successful sexual relationships, and has now met a man whom she wants to marry.

Laura's success story shows how disabling inhibitions should be dealt with. You need to face your fears, instead of running away from them. But in most cases, you'll need support from other people to help you to do this.

---

inhibitions about

stripping

As mentioned in the last chapter, many people are very inhibited about taking off their clothes in front of someone else, and there are a number of women and men whose partners have never seen them naked.

Partly this inhibition is due to early childhood conditioning. Only recently, I heard a three-year-old screaming the place down because she didn't want her grandmother to see her with no clothes on. The children of nudist families tend to grow up refreshingly free of this inhibition.

The other factor is that many people are embarrassed about the defects in their bodies — or what they think are imperfections. For instance, a lot of men are reluctant to be seen naked because they have a bit of paunch. And many women are terrified of being seen nude because they think their breasts are saggy, or because they have spots on their bottoms (a very common condition).

Reluctance to strip off can seriously damage your sex life — particularly if your inhibition starts to irritate your partner. To put things right, you have to confront the problem, as the following case history shows.

Joanna was a pretty girl, who was very popular with boys. But every sex relationship that she entered into went wrong — for one very simple reason.

Although she was willing enough to have sexual relations with a man if she liked him, she never, ever allowed one to see her breasts. She insisted that they remained covered at all times and even wore a bra during intercourse.

Not surprisingly, man after man simply dropped her. Even though they liked her, they weren't interested in a girl who wouldn't show her breasts. This succession of rejections made Joanna quite depressed, and she began to despair of ever marrying and settling down.

The remedy. **One night Joanna talked to a girlfriend about her problem. After a while, the friend asked: 'Do you think your hang-up could be connected with the fact that your mother died of breast cancer when you were tiny?'**

That was it. Joanna realized that when she was three, she'd known that the tragedy of her mother's death had somehow been caused by breast trouble. The fears about breasts which this episode had imbued in her had stayed with her through the years, although she hadn't consciously been aware of it.

She spent the next few weeks talking the matter through with her friend, and gradually she came to see that her breasts could be objects of beauty and pleasure, rather than fear.

Eventually, she was able to let the love of her life look at, kiss and fondle her breasts without any uneasy feelings at all.

---

inhibitions about

keeping the light on

Quite a few people won't make love if the light is still on. This can be very off-putting for a partner who wants to have the benefit of seeing his/her loved one's face and body during intercourse.

The origins of this inhibition are the same as those about stripping and if you want to defeat the problem, you have to confront it.

CASE HISTORY

Bill was an older man who'd been divorced for many years. He met a new woman, fell in love with her, and wanted to marry her. She was really lusty in bed, and they always had a great time making love. But she was puzzled and hurt by the fact that he always insisted on putting out the light before sex. She wondered if it was something he didn't like about her.

The remedy. **Eventually, she got Bill to talk about it. He reluctantly explained that his first wife had once hurt him deeply by saying that he 'looked silly during his climax'. Since then, he'd always felt that he would appear a figure of fun if he left the light on.**

His new lover reassured him that she certainly wouldn't find him foolish-looking, and that in fact she wanted to see him coming. Then, over a period of weeks, she got him to experiment with having a romantic candle-light in the bedroom. From there, they moved on to a low side-light with a coloured bulb — and finally Bill was able to enjoy sex even when the full overhead light was on. He was cured.

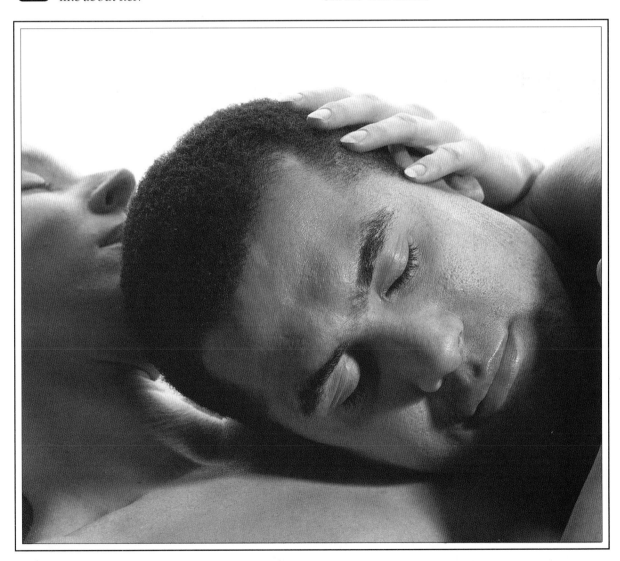

● Once inhibitions have been overcome, sex can be much more fulfilling for both partners.

inhibitions about touching sex organs

These inhibitions are surprisingly common. For instance, there are quite a few men around who have great difficulty in persuading themselves to touch their partner's vagina or clitoris. Clearly, men who suffer from this hang-up are not going to be successful lovers.

Once again, the origins of this inhibition lie in early training that certain parts of the body are 'dirty'. Furthermore, men who won't touch the vagina have often been brought up with the idea that women and their sex organs are to be feared in some way. It is very common to be frightened of the unknown, but, as with all sexual inhibitions, it is possible to put things right.

CASE HISTORY Sarah was 24 and married to Tony, who suffered from premature ejaculation. He went to a sex clinic, where they explained the simple squeeze grip which Sarah could apply in order to help him.

Unfortunately, Sarah — like a number of women — 'could not possibly' touch a man's penis with her hand. The couple were now stuck in an impasse, because there was no way that Tony could be cured of his PE — unless, of course, he found another partner who could do the squeeze grip on him.

The remedy. **Tony eventually persuaded Sarah to go along to the sex clinic with him. There, an understanding female doctor counselled her for a number of hours during which she helped her to see that her fear of the penis was irrational. Gradually, Sarah came round to the idea of touching the organ that she dreaded — and even found herself enjoying it.**

After some months, she was able to play with Tony's penis quite happily. She was also able to use the squeeze grip to help him cure his premature ejaculation.

inhibitions about naming sex organs

Good sex largely depends on men and women being able to talk to their lovers about their likes and dislikes. However, many couples find it difficult to communicate during love-making because they have no way of telling each other what they want.

Surprising though this may sound, the reason is that they can't bring themselves to say the words which describe the sex organs. In society, there's still a general consensus against speaking out loud the words which describe the 'naughty bits'. So it's not unusual for the bedtime conversation of some couples to be confined to embarrassed mutterings like:

'Shall I rub your . . . er . . . er?'
'Would you mind not pressing so hard on my . . . ahem . . . thingy?'

These problems stem from the repressive attitudes of a generation ago, when words like 'penis', 'vagina' and 'clitoris' could not be printed in newspapers or magazines. Almost unbelievably, they didn't appear in many dictionaries either. So, most people grew up having only a limited knowledge of sex words. Those words they did know could be divided into three categories:

(1) *'Baby talk'* words, which had been used (often reluctantly) by their parents. Very often, these words would be incomprehensible to anyone except close relatives, since they'd been passed down the family.

(2) *'School playground'* expressions, which were learned surreptitiously from classmates. Children who were overheard using these terms were usually punished because the words were regarded by teachers as crude and vulgar.

(3) *Proper medical expressions*, derived from Latin or Greek. Unfortunately, these 'correct' terms are not all that widely known even today. Furthermore, most people mispronounce them hopelessly and know they're mispronouncing them, so adding to their embarrassment and confusion.

What a mess! Things are improving in what has become a more open and free-speaking society, but there are still many people who suffer dreadfully from inhibitions about 'naming of parts', as this case history shows.

CASE HISTORY

Andrea was 29, and her sex life with her husband Peter was in a shambles — mainly because both of them were far too inhibited about sex words to be able to communicate in bed.

Andrea hardly ever reached orgasm, because she needed lots of clitoral stimulation to achieve the big 'O'. She wished she could ask Peter to stimulate her clitoris, but she'd only seen the word written down once, and she was deeply embarrassed about the fact that she had no idea how to pronounce it.

Peter was almost as bad. He kept coming too quickly because Andrea twitched her vagina just as he was getting excited — with the result that he went over the top too soon. But he was quite incapable of saying to her 'Please don't twitch your vagina so soon, darling', because the only word he knew for vagina was 'foo-foo' (a legitimate local term) — and he felt silly calling it that but didn't know what else to say.

The remedy. **By good fortune, Andrea heard through a friend about an organization called 'Sexual Attitude Restructuring' or 'SAR'. It's based in California, but holds seminars from time to time in Britain. Andrea's friend told her that it was sexually liberating, so Andrea dragged Peter along one weekend.**

They found themselves sitting in a room with about 20 other people who had gone along to try to free themselves from sexual hang-ups. Various techniques to release inhibitions were employed by the seminar leader, and the following one worked really well for Peter and Andrea.

The leader stood in front of a blackboard, and invited the audience to call out every rude word they knew. She wrote all these words on the board, and the seminar then discussed their actual meaning in great detail.

Three hours of this shock treatment not only enlarged Andrea and Peter's vocabulary enormously, but also had a dramatic effect in making them feel less inhibited about sexy words. From then on, they had no difficulty whatsoever in telling each other what they wanted in bed.

---

inhibitions about

masturbation

It's possible that more people have hang-ups about masturbation than any other sexual topic. Certainly, my 'problem page' postbag is full of letters from men and women who have the most colossal guilt about wanking — the common slang term for this.

This is not surprising, really, because it's not all that long since adults told youngsters that it would damage their eyes or make hair grow on their palms. For much of this century, masturbation was regarded as 'the secret vice', or self-abuse.

Only in about the 1960s — when the so-called Permissive Society came on the scene — did it become just about permissible to say in print that virtually all men masturbated at some time. In the late 1970s, I remember saying in an article that much the same was true of women. The result was a cacophony of protest from a large number of readers — mostly men — who thought it was outrageous that a doctor should dare to suggest that women ever indulged in 'this filthy and dangerous habit'. Things are different twenty years later and the following is now public knowledge:

- Masturbation (male or female) isn't dangerous — it's totally harmless, and can in fact improve a couple's sex life.
- The vast majority of men and women have enjoyed masturbating — or touching themselves — at some time.
- Many men and women masturbate throughout their lives.

- Masturbation frequently forms part of the love play between couples.
- Using masturbation with your lover in this way can often be liberating for both of you.

Gail was 18 and a virgin. She'd just met a really nice guy with whom she hoped she would have a long-term relationship. He urged her to go along with him to a clinic where they could get some contraception, so that they could start making love as soon as possible.

But Gail was strangely reluctant. She kept finding excuses not to go the clinic, saying things like 'I wouldn't mind if I didn't have to be examined by the doctor'.

Eventually, her boyfriend persuaded her to explain. It emerged that Gail had been masturbating to orgasm for several years, and was afraid that the clinic doctor would realize this fact, and reprimand her for so doing.

The remedy. **Gail's boyfriend told her that he was really turned on by the idea of her masturbating. Furthermore, when she finally agreed to go to the clinic, she was interviewed by a friendly woman medical officer who told her that there was now evidence that women who have masturbated are likely to have more satisfying sex lives than women who haven't. Gail immediately stopped worrying.**

inhibitions about

oral sex

Before we move on to these inhibitions, it should be understood that oral sex doesn't appeal to everyone — and if a couple don't want to practise it, there's obviously no reason why they should.

- Knowing how to masturbate will help you to enjoy a more full and satisfying sex life.

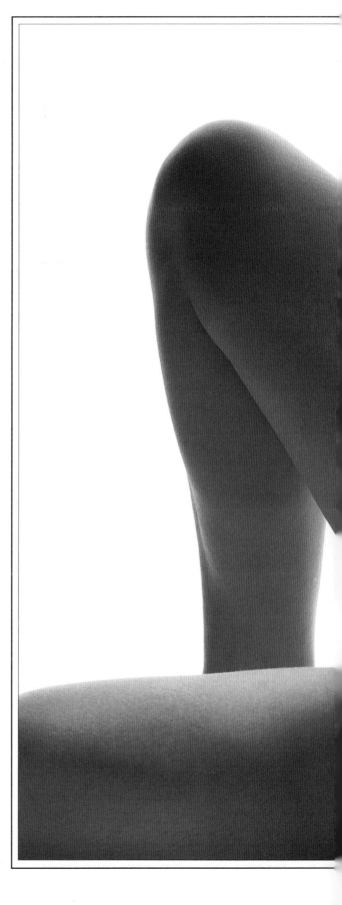

However, an increasing proportion of men and women do go in for oral caresses these days. Problems may arise if, for example, a woman has had great satisfaction from oral stimulation in a previous relationship, but then becomes involved with a man who refuses to provide it for her. In such circumstances, it would be wise for the man to try to overcome his inhibitions.

There are actually two kinds of inhibitions about oral sex: inhibitions about receiving it; and inhibitions about giving it.

inhibitions about receiving it

A man may feel inhibited about receiving oral sex from a woman because he genuinely fears that she will bite his penis. A woman may fear receiving oral sex because she may think that she doesn't smell very nice or look very nice 'down below'.

Both sexes may be worried about receiving oral sex because they fear they might fart near their lover's face — an embarrassing prospect indeed!

inhibitions about giving it

Women may be wary of giving oral sex because they're afraid that the penis might choke them, or because they dislike the appearance and taste of seminal fluid. Men may dislike giving oral sex because they have fears about the vagina, or can't cope with its exotic smell and taste.

If one of a couple does have any of these worries, then it's important that the two of them should talk things through and discuss how they feel about it all, as our example shows.

CASE HISTORY

Ian and Elaine were divorced people who met when they were in their 50s. They fell in love, and soon moved in together, enjoying very agreeable sex most of the time.

But there was a slight problem. Ian had always been given oral sex by his previous girlfriends, and he was puzzled and hurt when Elaine didn't want to do the same for him. He feared that she thought he wasn't clean, and spent ages washing himself before every sexual encounter — all to no avail.

The remedy. **They sat down and talked it out. Elaine's previous husband had forced oral sex on her, and at her age she didn't want to be reminded of all that trauma. She was, however, willing to do all sorts of other nice things in bed for Ian.**

Having heard this, Ian realized that although he'd assumed that oral sex was 'part of the service', he'd never really derived that much pleasure from it. After some consideration, he reckoned he could take it or leave it, and so from then on, they left oral sex out of their love-making.

how inhibitions have changed

Sexual inhibitions have changed dramatically during the last hundred years. At the turn of the century, the world was shrouded in a fog of repression and inhibition as far as sexual matters were concerned. The Austrian psychoanalyst Sigmund Freud (1856–1939) was the first to realize the extent to which people's lives were being crippled by sexual inhibition. As the century progressed, men and women began to throw off the restraints imposed on what they could think, say or do — in private and in public.

Most sociological experts seem to think that there is at least some truth in the popular view that people became significantly less inhibited during the 1920s (when life became less constrained after the First World War), and in the 1960s (the decade of the

● As people gain more maturity and experience they tend to become far less inhibited in bed.

Permissive Society). The contraceptive pill and many other social factors have played major parts in making society less sexually inhibited than it was. But there are still many men and women whose sex lives are not as good as they could be because they carry an unnecessary burden of inhibition.

how inhibitions
change with age

Young people often assume that their elders are sexually inhibited. This is nonsense as a rule. (However, it's true that, because of the way she was brought up, a woman born in the 1930s is likely to be more inhib-

ited in bed than a girl born in, say, 1975 — though this wouldn't invariably be the case.) In general, people do not become more sexually inhibited as they grow older. In fact, the reverse is often true.

As people grow more mature, they should gradually develop a wider experience and a deeper understanding of life. This is what happens in many cases. As a doctor, I have seen a lot of people who were anxious about sex when they were in their 20s, but who became much more relaxed and easygoing about it when they reached their 40s.

This is particularly true of women, who often find it difficult to lie back and 'let go' when they're teenagers. But by their middle years, they are often having orgasms as though there were no tomorrow. It's worth reminding yourself that inhibitions don't have to stay with you for life and it's quite possible to leave them behind you.

OVERCOMING INHIBITIONS

The case histories in this chapter show some of the ways in which inhibitions can be dealt with. But before you (or your partner) can tackle a personal inhibition, you must first admit its existence and identify what is causing the problem.

Next, try to sort out whether you actually need to get rid of the inhibition. To take just one example, if your lover wants you to do something that's very distasteful to you, maybe you shouldn't give in. Maybe your inhibition is actually right for you, or maybe it isn't. You need to decide this for yourself.

Communication is nearly always the best starting point when trying to resolve a sexual problem. In general, you should begin by talking openly with your partner. It may also help if you discuss things with good friends or relatives whom you trust.

You may also find it necessary to consult a professional: for example, a Family Planning Clinic, a doctor, a nurse, a psychologist, a marriage guidance or youth counsellor, or a sex therapist. Remember that they will also probably have some inhibitions of their own and it's more than likely that they've already helped others overcome similar inhibitions.

Whatever you do, try to keep an open mind, and don't rush things. You may feel a good deal more relaxed about your inhibition in a few months' time, but it may take much longer.

So, just begin gradually! In most cases it's best to tackle your sexual inhibitions very slowly — if possible breaking the problem down into smaller compartments.

The classic example of this 'gradualization' process would be the case of a man who cannot bear the thought of being seen naked by anyone even by his long-term lover. It would be very difficult for him to confront his inhibition by simply whipping all his clothes off, which could be a highly traumatic experience!

But let's imagine that one day he lets his partner see his toes, and finds out that's not too bad. Next day he exposes his feet, and the day after that his ankles — and so on, very gradually indeed.

tips to help an inhibited relationship

Here are five simple things which you can do if you're in a badly inhibited relationship with your partner and you want to improve the situation.

1 Treat yourself to a peaceful, quiet time in which you can be on your own in comfortable, warm, sensuous surroundings (like a bed or bath). Lie back, think relaxed, sexy thoughts, and gently masturbate. It's OK — you're allowed to enjoy it.

2 This may not always be easy but persuade your partner to let you do the same thing in front of him/her.

3 Encourage him/her to masturbate you in exactly the same way that you have demonstrated as being comfortable and pleasant for you.

4 Now ask him/her to masturbate in front of you — demonstrating to you the movements and pressures that are most agreeable.

5 Use those same movements and pressures on your partner, asking for continuous guidance as to what's best.

All this may take you many weeks or months. Don't rush it — a good sexual relationship isn't usually built in a day.

Note: Although we've stressed in this chapter that severe inhibitions are best dealt with gradually, it is worth mentioning that psychologists sometimes treat disabling phobias by subjecting the sufferer to very sudden exposure to them. The idea is that when the person is abruptly and totally exposed to the situation they fear, then they'll get all the trauma over with very rapidly and (with luck) be cured. However, this is a risky technique and no- one should use it except under the control of an expert.

Would you describe yourself as. . . ?

— *women*

— *men*

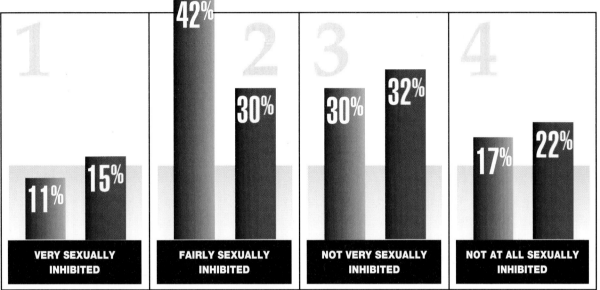

42% **30%** **30%** **32%** **17%** **22%** **11%** **15%**

1	2	3	4
VERY SEXUALLY INHIBITED	FAIRLY SEXUALLY INHIBITED	NOT VERY SEXUALLY INHIBITED	NOT AT ALL SEXUALLY INHIBITED

● 45% of men and 53 % of women say they are very or fairly sexually inhibited.

Which of the following things, if any, help you to be less inhibited in bed?

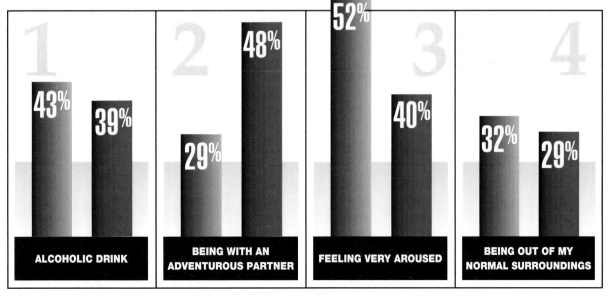

1	2	3	4
43% / 39%	29% / 48%	52% / 40%	32% / 29%
ALCOHOLIC DRINK	BEING WITH AN ADVENTUROUS PARTNER	FEELING VERY AROUSED	BEING OUT OF MY NORMAL SURROUNDINGS

● Nearly a third of men and women find a change of scene a liberating factor.

4

Sexual Performance

*t*oday, society is undoubtedly preoccupied with the sexual performances of both men and women alike. Prurient questions on the prowess of the famous are put to their ex-lovers on TV chat shows and newspapers frequently entice their readers with ridiculous headlines like:

> *MY LOVER DID IT SIX TIMES A NIGHT, SAYS BIMBO!*
>
> *SOAP STAR WAS 'INSATIABLE' CLAIMS EX-LOVER!*
>
> *SOCCER STAR'S WILLY WAS 'PATHETIC' REVEALS PORN QUEEN!*

Although this performance-orientated nonsense, in which people are judged by how well they score in bed, has no relevance to real life or having a good relationship, sexual performance is still sometimes rated according to a list of misconceived prerequisites. Whether or not you are assumed to be a good lover might depend on the following:

for men:

- How readily you can get an erection.
- How big it is.
- How long you can keep it up.
- How far you can push it up.
- How hard you can thrust.
- Most importantly, how many times a night you can perform!

for women:

- Are you 'ready for it' at all times?
- Are you a 'real goer' (whatever that means)?
- Do you immediately moisten at the drop of a pair of trousers?
- Do you climax at precisely the same time as your lovers?
- Do you have multiple orgasms — one after another in succession?
- Do you give wonderful 'hand jobs'?
- Do you also give expert 'blow jobs'?
- Do you scream and shout in bed, constantly begging for more?

I hope you can see that these sort of sexual standards for men and women are quite ludicrous. You could say that they're a bit of harmless fun, but today's performance-obsessed attitude to sexuality has a very definite down side.

Many men and women feel very inadequate as lovers because they haven't a hope of competing with the alleged 'standards' mentioned above. It's quite common for men to feel depressed and

● A woman should simply enjoy her sex life without worrying about whether her performance reaches an imaginary standard.

● Laughter, tenderness and companionship in bed are far more important than worrying about performance.

miserable about their sexuality because they know that they can't measure up to the bedtime performance of fictional heroes like James Bond. Similarly, a lot of women lose all confidence in their sexuality because they're aware that they can't match the bizarre antics of heroines in erotic fiction. Their sexuality is a highly sensitive area for most people and what would be dismissed as mere fantasy were it pertaining to another subject can be very easily taken on board as fact when it comes to sex.

The truth about sexual performance is often not at all what people imagine, though there are certain levels of sexual ability which a man or woman can reasonably expect to 'achieve' at various ages. But it's more important to remember that there is no need to compete with the popular sexual standards which are frequently written about but which in reality are largely mythical.

When love-making, it's far more important to enjoy mutual warmth, tenderness, love, cuddles, companionship and laughter than to worry about standards of performance.

PRESSURE on MEN to PERFORM

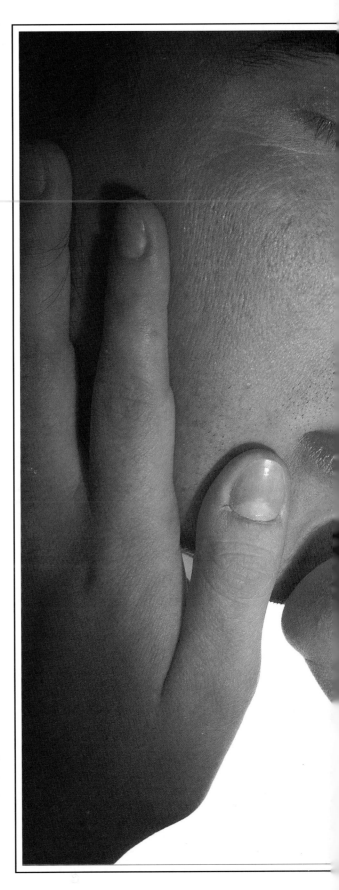

To a large extent, it is men (not women) who create the enormous pressure on males to perform well in bed. One reason for this is that men are the principal readers of ever-popular erotic novels and semi-pornographic magazines. The performance of men and the sex described in these publications is far removed from reality. But although intelligent men must realize this (the literature is designed to titillate, after all), this still puts a niggling fear into some men that they should try to match their sexual performance to the fantasies they've read about.

It doesn't in fact matter what the source is for these myths about prodigious virility. The point is that a man who is exposed to this nonsense may well feel that he has much to live up to. If he can 'only' make love once a night — and that perhaps with difficulty — he's liable to feel that he's not as good a man as he should be. But he's making a false judgement and should instead be concentrating on realistic expectations for men at various ages (see pages 78–9).

It's true, however, that throughout history, men have been under considerable pressure to perform. This is because women can have intercourse without trying — but men can't. A couple simply cannot have full sexual intercourse unless the man can achieve an erection, and having an erection is not always easy.

In the last few years, there has been a new, increased pressure on men, caused by the expectations of women. Until a generation ago, it seems that the majority of women wanted remarkably little from sex, and were resigned to accept the fact that sex is not always wonderful. But today— and quite rightly so — the average woman expects her partner to be good in bed. With perfect justification, she feels that he should be required to treat her considerately, to give her a reasonable amount of foreplay, and to help her to reach orgasm.

● Today, women expect far more love play from their lovers than they once would have done.

Not all men can cope with these female expectations. Sex experts who counsel young men are now reporting that they're seeing a number of clients who are desperately worried that they're simply 'not good enough' for their girlfriends or fiancées. So it's clearly very important that today's woman should try to reassure and encourage her partner, and not put excessive pressure on him. He's already getting quite enough of that from the media — and very possibly from his own friends.

PRESSURE on WOMEN to PERFORM

Women have also come under increasing pressure to perform well sexually in recent years. Within living memory, all that was requested of many wives was that they should allow their husbands to have sex with them on a preordained night once a week. Things have changed dramatically, and it's now acknowledged that a woman deserves a good sex life as much as a man.

Interestingly, very little of this pressure has come from the women themselves. Although they do sometimes discuss their sex lives and relationships with their friends, there is no competitive element among women, whereas men tend to boast about their sexual performance. If a woman's sex life is going well for her, then her friends are pleased, though possibly sometimes jealous. No, in the case of women, pressures mainly come from two sources: the media, and men.

The media. While women's magazines have played an important role in educating women about their bodies and their sexuality, they do sometimes raise slightly unrealistic expectations — particularly by suggesting that everyone is having a wonderful sex life, so you should be too.

Perhaps rather more potent is the romantic/ slightly erotic popular fiction that many women read: the majority of its heroines are good at sex, and have no trouble responding to the amorous advances of the hero or villain. There are few modern romances in which the leading character has difficulties in

reaching her climax. Yet in real life, most women find themselves in this situation from time to time.

Even more unrealistic are the sexy, semi-pornographic magazines and books which some men bring home and very frequently ask women to look at with them. These publications create ludicrous views of male sexuality — with throbbing cocks having 15 climaxes on every page — and the view they present of female sexuality is equally absurd. In these books and magazines, all women are 'thirsting for sex' or 'desperate for action'. They climax again and again; they don't ask for foreplay, tenderness or love because apparently they need none of these things. All these fictional women want is a series of penises thrust into them repeatedly — plus endless bouts of rampaging oral sex with regiments of insatiable men, and a spot of lesbianism and sado-masochism when life gets dull.

The fact is that women are not at all like the characters on the printed page. But although women realize that these fictional women are deliberately playing to male fantasies, they may still may feel that they aren't as good at sex as they should be.

Men. There are various ways in which men put pressure on women — for instance, aggressive or insensitive remarks like:

- 'If you really loved me, you'd do that for me.'
- 'My last girlfriend was a lot quicker off the mark than you.'
- 'Haven't you come yet?'
- 'I never had any complaints before, darling.'
- 'You're not a lesbian, are you?'
- 'Why can't you come without so much foreplay?'
- 'You seem to be very dry — are you menopausal?'
- 'Sorry: I assumed you'd finish as quickly as me.'

● Women should not allow men to pressurize them in bed — a good lover is considerate, not demanding.

In fairness to men, most of them don't mean any real harm by these thoughtless remarks, which are usually made out of ignorance rather than malice. If you're a woman, try to remember that men — especially young men — often have the most incredibly naive or misinformed ideas about female sexuality. In particular, they may find it extremely hard to grasp the fact that women can't just switch on an instant sexual response in the way that men usually can.

To sum up, don't let yourself be pressurized by any man's view of what you 'should' be doing in bed — you'll never have a truly enjoyable sex life like that. Frankly, he's rather unlikely to know what he's talking about — but be tactful about the way you express this to him!

unrealistic and realistic expectations: men

Now let's compare myth with reality. As the American expert Dr Bernard Zilbergeld says, the popular and enduring myth about the human male is that he has a penis that is 'two foot long, hard as steel, and goes all night'. The reality is that the penis is a very soft anatomical structure which spends only a small part of its existence in a reasonably firm condition.

When comparing expectations with real life, it's helpful to look at various aspects of male sexuality, such as a man's erection, orgasm, ejaculation and expertise.

erection

Myth. **A man should be able to get a hard-on whenever he wants to and keep it going all day and all night, if necessary. Furthermore, in order for the man to qualify as really 'virile', the erection should be so vertical that the man's organ is practically touching his belly.**

FACT Most younger men can indeed reach an erection most of the time when they want to. But if they're nervous — for instance, with a new partner — it can often be very difficult.

As a man gets older, he really cannot expect to be able to produce an erection at a moment's notice. Although most males are potent beyond the age of 70, the number of erections which they have per day tends to diminish gradually but steadily through life.

The myth that the penis should stand up vertically during all erections was long ago debunked by scientists. Dr Alfred Kinsey — author of Sexual Behavior in the Human Male (1948, the so-called 'Kinsey Report') — found that only 8–10 per cent of males 'carry the erect penis nearly vertically, more or less tightly against the belly'. He added 'the average position, calculated from all ages, is very slightly above the horizontal'.

So, if yours sticks out horizontally there is no need to fret — you're perfectly normal.

orgasm

Myth. **Real men should be able to come time after time, with no limit to the number of orgasms they can have during a love-making session.**

FACT Kinsey discovered that only in males under 15 is multiple orgasm of this sort at all possible (and in fact, only 20 per cent of them can do it).

The vast majority of adult males cannot climax more than once in an hour, except under the most extreme sexual stimulation. This is because the

AGE	AVERAGE NUMBER OF ORGASMS	AGE	AVERAGE NUMBER OF ORGASMS
15	4	40	2
20	3	45	2.1
25	2.9	50	2
30	2.5	55	1.5
35	2.1	60	1

● This table shows the average total of male climaxes per week at various ages.

male sex apparatus needs a considerable period of time to recover after an orgasm. This necessary recovery time means that men are actually capable of far fewer orgasms than women, who are able to reach orgasm repeatedly.

In practice, the number of orgasms which a sexually active man is likely to have in a lifetime is far less than you might think from reading erotic novels with their super-virile heroes.

ejaculation

Myth. **Books describing sex scenes often speak of men producing vast rivers of fluid when they come. The publicity material for some of the pornographic videos which are now openly on sale also perpetuates this myth. ('The heroic warrior pumps out nearly a pint of semen as six beautiful girls fight each other for the privilege of lapping it up.')**

FACT As mentioned earlier, Mr Average produces just one teaspoon of seminal fluid when he climaxes.

expertise

Myth. **Everybody is supposed to be a great lover these days; heroes in books are invariably expert at love-making — though curiously enough, they rarely spend time on foreplay. Fictional heroes seem to be able to induce tumultuous and multiple orgasms in women without any problem.**

FACT In real life, very few women will reach orgasm simply by having a penis pumping hard inside them. The great majority will require a great deal more care and attention than that — including plenty of foreplay.

In practice, most men are not great experts at sexual techniques. But it is reasonable for a woman to expect her lover to try to develop at least some expertise in bed, and to learn some love play caresses which will give her pleasure.

unrealistic and realistic expectations: women

Next, let's compare myth with reality as far as women are concerned. Here, it's worth looking at four different areas: enthusiasm, lubrication, orgasm and expertise.

enthusiasm

Myth. **The story which many men, and some women, have swallowed hook, line and sinker is this. Females are ravenous sexual creatures, who are desperate to have a penis inside them at every possible moment. Books which describe women making love with wild abandon are partly to blame for perpetuating this myth.**

FACT It is true that some women occasionally behave like lust-crazed heroines. But women are nowhere near as obsessed with sex as the male myth wants them to be. Unlike men, they tend not to think about sex dozens of times every hour. Very sensibly, they have other things on their minds.

In practice, it is reasonable to expect a woman to show a fair amount of enthusiasm for love-making, when she's ready for it. But men should bear in mind that women are not always in the mood for sex: some days they feel very randy, on others they don't.

One final point about female enthusiasm for sex: you can't expect your partner to show much of it unless you (the male) spend a good deal of time and effort in making her feel wanted, treasured, and loved.

lubrication

Myth. **Men like to think that women are always 'wet and ready'. In some novels the heroines pour out such vast quantities of love juices that it's a wonder** that **their lovers don't nearly get** drowned in the ensuing flood.

FACT The idea that women are always 'wet and ready' is as ridiculous as saying that men are always 'erect and ready'. (Lubrication, as we have seen, is basically the female equivalent of erection.)

Most women's vaginas tend to be fairly dry — depending to some extent, however, on what time of the month it is. When they become sexually excited, it usually takes them several minutes before they can produce any worthwhile degree of lubrication. So men should bear in mind that:

■ You shouldn't rush things.
■ You must try to induce lubrication by romancing her, spending time on foreplay and caressing her well before you try to enter.
■ It may be worth investing in one of the excellent vaginal lubricants, such as K-Y Jelly, which are now sold by most chemists. Do remember, though, some women may be offended if you suggest that a little artificial vaginal lubrication might help, so choose your words carefully.

Two further points to note:

■ After the menopause, many women do become quite dry and may find it extremely hard to lubricate even when they're sexually aroused. If the above-mentioned vaginal lubricants don't help, then the answer is usually to consult a doctor and discuss the possibility of using a vaginal hormone cream. This vaginal version of hormone replacement therapy (HRT) ishighly effective — but there is a slight risk that the man will absorb a little through his penis. In practice, there should be no real difficulty as long as you don't put the female hormone cream in just before intercourse.
■ In recent years, it has been shown that a small proportion of women do gush a special sex fluid at the moment of orgasm. For

ages, doctors (myself included) refused to believe this, but it has now been proven. These women appear to be producing fluid from a mysterious structure which may be the equivalent of the male's prostate gland. The amount of fluid pumped out varies, but it's often more than a man produces.

orgasm

Myth. **All real women are orgasmic from a very early age; they come the first time they ever have intercourse. Furthermore, they have multiple orgasms from the word go, and are liable to reel off several dozen climaxes as soon a man enters them.**

FACT Most women find it difficult to reach orgasm when they're young — but they do tend to find it much easier as they grow older and more experienced.

However, some women do indeed learn how to climax at a very early age, particularly if they masturbate as teenagers. But from one huge sex survey which I conducted quite recently, it emerged that the average woman didn't reach orgasm until about two years after she first had intercourse. Very, very few reported that they came on the night they lost their virginity.

What about the famous multiple orgasm — in other words, more than one orgasm in a session? The truth is that until recent years, these were quite rare. In Sexual Behavior in the Human Female (1953), Dr Kinsey reported that only 14 per cent of women could have multiple orgasms. But as women have become more sexually liberated, and as men have learned how to stimulate women better, things have changed. My own studies of women's magazine readers have suggested that about 60 per cent of women are having multiple orgasms these days, and recent research work in America has produced similar figures.

Most encouragingly, my own surveys show that women are much more likely to have multiple orgasms as they grow older. The highest incidence of multiple orgasm is in the over-45s.

To induce vaginal lubrication, a man should spend time on foreplay with his partner before attempting to enter her.

Summing up, what can a man reasonably expect 'orgasm-wise' from his partner? Well, nothing at all — unless he really appreciates her, encourages her and makes her feel good. Most important, he should spend time on foreplay and try to stimulate her with techniques that will help her to come.

Even if he does all these things, he must remember three points.

- There may well be days when she just doesn't feel like climaxing .
- If she's young and relatively inexperienced, it may well be some considerable period of time before her body becomes totally comfortable with the process of climax — let alone multiple climax.
- Many women (possibly even the majority) go through episodes in their lives when they just aren't interested in climaxing for a while. This very commonly happens in the weeks after childbirth. To try to force a woman into orgasm against her will at such times would be extremely insensitive and probably a waste of time.

expertise

Myth. **Many men think that women should be tremendously clever in bed, and skilled at all sorts of erotic techniques, so that they can give a man mind-blowing satisfaction all the time.**

FACT Young, inexperienced women must by definition know next to nothing about sexual techniques. In reality, women need practice and to learn by experience before they become really skilled in such matters as giving a good 'hand job' or 'blow job', so don't expect it of them.

If you are in a long-term, loving relationship, then it's reasonable to expect your female partner to learn gradually how to please you in bed — in just the same way as you will learn how to please her.

If you don't anticipate perfect sex the first time you make love, then you won't be disappointed — and you may be pleasantly surprised.

why are men expected to take the lead?

There's one special pressure which applies to men and not to women. In society, men have traditionally been expected to be the first to suggest a date and to take the lead in bed. As far as sex is concerned, taking the lead means things like:

- Giving the first indication that you want intercourse to take place.
- Physically making the first move towards the bedroom.
- Starting to remove clothes (from either partner).
- Being the first to touch the other person intimately.
- Suggesting (or perhaps deciding) what love play techniques are going to be used.
- Making the move to start intercourse.
- Effectively determining the 'end point' of intercourse — by coming.

All this decision-making can make life quite difficult for some men, particularly if they are very young or by nature shy or diffident. For instance, a man may feel very awkward expressing himself, and even if he wants to have sex, he may be at a loss to know what best to say or do to initiate it or how to do something (like taking off a woman's bra) without being clumsy.

In recent years, there has been a recognition of the fact that for men always to decide exactly what's going to happen in love-making is a ridiculous way to carry on. More and more women are rebelling against that tradition, saying very firmly what they want to do in bed — and then going ahead and doing it.

Many women find that sex is more stimulating and satisfying if they take the initiative more often when love-making. Some — less liberated — men may not like it, but the majority of men will react favourably when they hear their woman say the following phrases:

Men have traditionally been expected to take the lead, for example by initiating undressing.

It's well worth trying the 'doggy position' if it appeals to you, but don't be pressurized into it.

- I think we should make love tonight.
- It's time we took our clothes off.
- Just put your hand here, darling, will you?
- Lie back and relax while I do something nice to you.
- I want you inside me.
- Please don't 'come' just yet — I want to keep going like this for a while.
- I'm there — 'come' whenever you like.

performance and trying out positions

As society has become much more liberated in the last few years, a curious thing has happened. Because the Kama Sutra and similar books have become popular reading matter (and are even given to friends as wedding presents), it has become established that a good 'performer' in bed must necessarily be able to make love in hundreds of different positions.

Some enjoyable variation in position can indeed be very useful in keeping sex alive and enjoyable, as we'll see in Chapter Seven. But nobody should feel pressurized into having a repertoire of dozens of different positions up his or her sleeve just for the sake of it.

For most couples, being able to make love in two or three different positions is usually sufficient — with perhaps a change to certain particularly comfortable ones when the woman is pregnant. Older people whose movements are limited by arthritis or rheumatism often benefit greatly by trying out a new position, and the same is true of some handicapped people. Four of the most popular, comfortable positions that don't require any strenuous acrobatics are as follows:

'Mother Superior'. The woman simply lies on top of the man, with her legs between his. Because there is so little pressure on her abdomen, this position is thoroughly recommended for pregnancy.

'Doggy position'. Much to my surprise, this was the most popular with romantically minded women in one very large survey which I conducted. It's exactly as you would imagine from the (very unromantic) name: the woman kneels on all fours, and the man enters her from behind, kneeling between her calves.

'The Chair'. The man sits in a chair. His partner sits on his lap, facing away from him — and he enters her from below. As a variation, she can sit sideways across his lap.

'The Spoons'. In this very comfortable position, the couple lie on their side (man behind woman) snuggled up together like two spoons in a drawer. Again, he enters her from behind. This is particularly good during pregnancy or if one of you has arthritis of the hip.

the myth about simultaneous climax

There's one myth which the media (particularly books) keep perpetuating — and it can be a very harmful one. This is the myth of the simultaneous climax. If you relied on romantic or erotic fiction for your sex instruction, you would firmly believe that all couples are supposed to 'come' at the same time — every time they make love, of course. You are probably familiar with the sort of literature I'm talking about:

'A thousand skylarks fluttered within Arabella's heaving bosom as her passion mounted towards its highest point. Finally, as she reached the very zenith of desire, a wild moan burst from her lips. And at that very instant, Roderick too scaled the mighty pinnacle of love. As always, they had achieved the apogee of emotion at one and the same moment.'

Well, sometimes sex might be like that — but all modern sex surveys show that most of the time it is not. A number of people find this very hard to accept, but it's true. In the survey carried out for the Good Sex Guide TV series, we asked women to say how often they really did reach simultaneous orgasms with their partners (even including those who come simultaneously as a result of love play). The results were as follows:

- 45 per cent of women said that they achieved simultaneous climax either 'never' or 'rarely'.
- 41 per cent said that it happens 'most of the time'.
- Only 11 per cent said that it happens 'always' or 'almost every time'.

Summing up, simultaneous orgasm is very nice when it occurs, but at the moment, it happens only to a minority of couples all the time. However, the more you get to know your partner's needs, and the more you communicate, the more likely a simultaneous climax will be.

MYTHS ABOUT POTENCY

There's a widespread myth to the effect that a real red-blooded male can always produce an erection whenever it's required. But all men eventually discover that this is not true.

Every male will one day find himself in a situation when he just can't 'make it'. Unfortunately, many men panic when this happens to them; they fear they've developed some terrible disease or that this is the onset of life-long impotence. In the vast majority of cases, they are totally wrong.

However, there is a danger that a man may worry so much about his failure to get a hard-on that he will develop a real anxiety state. And it's a medical fact that anxiety produces chemicals which flow through your bloodstream and make it very difficult for you to get an erection.

In other words, if you get over-anxious about having failed to achieve an erection, you are in danger of creating a vicious circle, which really could prolong your potency problems.

● When you are having intercourse, don't worry too much about achieving simultaneous climax.

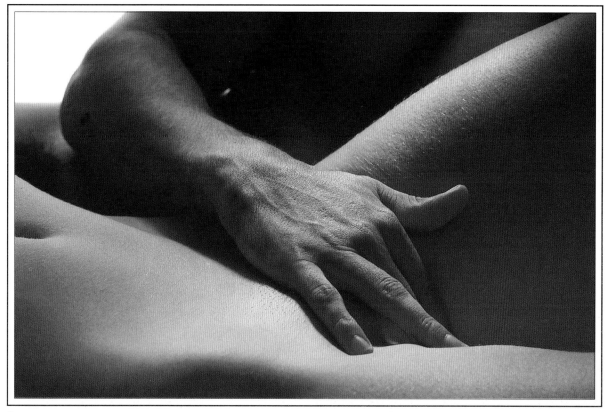

The majority of women require stimulation by hand as well to help them reach a climax.

In practical terms, what this means is that if you find that you can't make it one night, you should try very hard just to laugh at the fact that for once your body is too tired to produce an erection. It's very important to communicate with your partner, so that she can understand what's going on, and help you not to take it too seriously. If you don't tell her about it, it's quite possible she may feel scorned or hurt because suddenly you don't want to make love to her.

Remember that just because you can't get an erection doesn't mean that you can't satisfy her. Once the situation has been explained to them, most sensible and experienced women are only too pleased to be given satisfaction by their lover's lips, tongue and fingers, or to use a vibrator for a change.

Another common myth about erection failure is that if a man can't get a hard-on then he must be lacking in male hormones. This is just nonsense. As we'll see in a moment, it is very rare indeed for potency difficulties to be caused by a deficiency in testosterone (the male sex hormone).

FAILURE to REACH ERECTION

The main causes of occasional failure to reach erection are these:

- Tiredness
- Stress
- Worry
- Anxiety states
- Depression
- Drinking too much alcohol ('brewer's droop')
- Guilt (especially when trying to make love to somebody you shouldn't be in bed with!)
- Falling out of love/hostility to your partner

Longer term failure to reach erection can be caused by any of the above, but may also be due to:

- Blood pressure drugs and other

medication from a doctor
- Misuse of illegal drugs, such as heroin
- Excessive use of nicotine (from tobacco)
- Diabetes
- Nerve damage after major operations or severe injury
- Multiple sclerosis (MS)
- Most uncommonly, lack of male hormone

Some people may wonder whether age is also a factor. In the past, there has been a terrible tendency for doctors to say 'It must be your age, sir' — sometimes to people as young as 39 — and the patient has had to accept that. But the real truth is that in men, the decline in potency due to advancing age is far slower than many people imagine. To remind you, no less than 70 per cent of males are still potent at the age of 70.

impotence and how it can be cured

Impotence means recurrent failure to achieve a good enough erection for penetration of your partner. Possible causes are listed above, and if you're suffering from impotence, the first thing to do is to try to work out which of these causes applies to you.

The next step is to talk everything over with your partner, and see what she thinks about possible causes. This mutual discussion may be of great help. For instance, if you both feel that the main cause is tiredness, then your partner may well be able to help you by going to bed with you at a time when you've had a rest. She may also be able to assist you by giving a little gentle fellatio (oral sex) — since mouth suction is one of the best ways to bring a limp penis to full erection.

But if you can't cure the problem by your mutual efforts, then the next stage is to consult a professional. In Britain, I would recommend beginning by going, as a couple, to a Family Planning Clinic, simply because the doctors there probably have more experience of dealing with impotence than

anyone else. An alternative is to consult a Relate counsellor or a sex therapist. The main treatment which FP Clinics provide is commonsense counselling — often combined with the psychological methods developed by the American experts Masters and Johnson. Clearly, this will not be much help if you have a mainly physical cause for your impotence. In these circumstances, the Family Planning Medical Officer would probably suggest you consult a urologist.

A urologist is a surgeon who deals with the male sexual organs and the urinary organs of both males and females. In the last few years, two important new impotence treatments have become available — splints and injections.

Splints

A urologist can place a stiff or inflatable splint inside the tissue of your penis, so that you can make love if you want to. A stiff splint is just a rod, which gives you what amounts to a permanent erection. You simply point it upwards when you want to make love, and point it down again afterwards. An inflatable splint is one which you pump up by repeatedly pressing on a reservoir of fluid, often located in your scrotum. Having one of these splints inserted is quite a major procedure, and it carries some risks of going wrong. Also, you will almost certainly have to pay for the treatment.

It is now possible to buy an external splint (the Correctaid) which is really a thick condom with a suction tube attached. The idea is that you use the little tube to suck your penis into erection, and then make love with the device still on.

These external splints don't give you a lot of sensitivity and they are quite expensive (over £200 at the time of writing), but many men reckon that they're worth it.

Injections

Urologists (and a few family doctors) are now often willing to prescribe injections of powerful drugs which produce instant erection. The jab has to be given directly into the penis. The doctor may do it initially, and then give you the needles to take home and use yourself.

Like any other medical treatment, the injections can go wrong: the main possible side-effects are infection of the penis, bleeding, and an erection that won't go down. While the last eventuality may sound fine to many men, the fact is that such an erection is very painful. It necessitates a trip to hospital or a clinic to have it urgently deflated.

The most important thing to remember is that if you ever have problems with your sexual performance, there is nearly always a solution. If you are not in a permanent relationship, it may just be that you and your current lover are not the ideal couple. The good thing is that any new lover you become involved with won't know about your past sexual history, and you may well find, anyway, that your problems and insecurities vanish without too much effort on your behalf. Sex nearly always improves as you become more experienced at love-making.

How satisfied are you with your sex life at the moment?

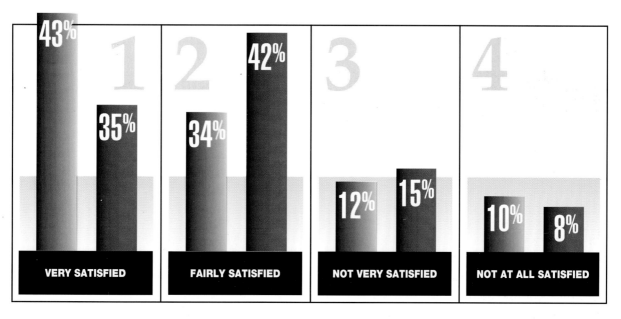

1	2	3	4
43% / 35%	34% / 42%	12% / 15%	10% / 8%
VERY SATISFIED	**FAIRLY SATISFIED**	**NOT VERY SATISFIED**	**NOT AT ALL SATISFIED**

● Nearly a quarter of men and women say they are not very or not at all satisfied with their sex life at the moment.

— *women*

— *men*

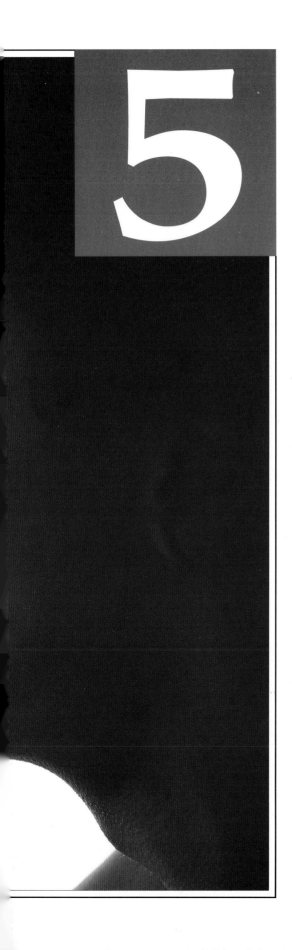

5

Sex with a New Partner – Etiquette and Attraction

*a*ttracting a new partner and having sex with him or her shouldn't just be a mechanical business. Books about human sexuality are liable to give the impression that love play and love-making are very technical activities: skills that you learn rather like fretwork or basketweaving.

Admittedly, it is vital to know about the basic mechanics of sex. But there's another side of sexuality that's often forgotten: its etiquette.

Yes, there is such a thing as 'sex etiquette'. All human societies have rules of behaviour which govern their various activities, and sex is no exception to this. There is a (so far largely unwritten) code which covers what you should and should not do when you form a new sexual relationship — and we'll be exploring that code in this chapter.

MANNERS and ETIQUETTE

If we had no system of rules governing our sex behaviour, life would be chaotic and probably miserable. I suppose that people would grab each other and 'do it' whenever they felt the urge — thinking only of their own sexual release, and never bothering about the consequences, or the happiness of the other person.

Fortunately, there is a code of manners (an etiquette) which indicates what we should do, especially when picking up a new sex partner and going to bed with her or him for the first time.

In Western society, the code varies slightly from country to country; for instance, it's still a lot more restrictive in Ireland than it is in England. But basically, the underlying principle is that you should show consideration for anybody with whom you're thinking of having sex, taking care not to cause him or her any hurt or embarrassment.

From first chatting up through first kiss to first petting to first intercourse, it's important to think about the other person's sexual needs and feel-   ings, and to try not to be selfish — however difficult it may be.

ATTRACTING a NEW PARTNER

Men and women approach the question of picking up a new partner in totally different ways — they don't look at the same features and their thoughts are not the same either.

what people see
when they meet

Let's look at the completely distinct ways in which men and women view a potential new partner.

Men. Males — especially when young — see a woman as a collection of physical features when they first clap eyes on her. As our survey shows, they tend immediately to latch on to a sexual part of the body, like breasts, legs, bottoms or lips. And, of course, they're keen on pretty faces.

Women. Females, on the other hand, usually take a less 'organ-orientated' view of a man whom they see in a street, café, disco or whatever. They tend to register him as a 'nice-looking' person or 'having a kind and humorous face' rather than wondering about the size of his penis. However, a substantial number of women do admit to being very attracted by the first sight of a man's bottom. If they really like it, they'll describe it in such terms as 'pert', 'neat', 'cute', 'tight', 'sweet', and 'worth getting hold of'. This is quite curious, since the bottom does not play a particularly major part in most people's love-making.

Women don't normally stare at a man's crotch when first introduced, although there is a small minority of women who find their eyes drawn to the bulge in a man's trousers when they're saying 'Hello'. (This may or may not be appreciated by the man!) The great majority of women, however, have their minds on other things.

what people think
when they meet

This brings us to the vital question of what is going through people's minds when they first meet. Here, the two sexes tend to misunderstand each other completely.

Men. When a man meets a potential new lover, something like this is likely to be running through of his mind:

- ■ 'Great tits! I wonder what the rest of her body's like. . . '
- ■ 'Terrific girl! I wouldn't mind giving her one. . . '
- ■ 'She's smiling at me! If I play my cards right, I might get my leg over.'

She's thinking about his mind and personality — but he's thinking about her body.

She is wondering 'Is he the one?' He is wondering 'Is she going to be good in bed?'

Note that the last statement is quite depersonalized: this particular man is scarcely thinking of the woman at all — what he is thinking about is getting himself into a 'leg-over situation'.

Not all men are quite as bad as this, but a vast amount are: within five minutes of meeting a woman, some Lotharios are already planning how they're going to ditch her with minimum fuss tomorrow morning!

Women. Male readers may perhaps imagine that when a woman meets a man, she is thinking to herself: 'What a stud! I'd really like to be fucked by him . . .'.

In fact, this is rarely the case. Although some women — particularly if they're feeling frustrated — do harbour such thoughts on first meeting a man, the fact is that more often than not a female will be thinking things like:

■ 'Isn't he wonderful . . .'
■ 'What a great body . . .'
■ 'He's fun to be with . . .'
■ 'I bet he's romantic and considerate . . .'
■ 'I wonder if he could be the big love of my life . . .'

So, whether you're male or female, do bear in mind that when you first meet a potential new partner the other person is probably thinking completely different thoughts from you. Two important points of etiquette emerge here:

■ If you're a man, don't imagine that any woman will be totally happy (and emotionally unaffected) if you cheerfully make love with her — and then dump her afterwards.
■ If you're a woman, don't make the common — and rather presumptuous — mistake of thinking that because he looks at you, he is considering some long-term romantic relationship. He may be, but the odds are that he's just undressing you with his eyes.

what people smell

when they meet

In recent years, it's become clear that smell plays a much larger part in physical attraction than we used to realize or admit.

At a first meeting, smells may cause sexual attraction (or the reverse) in three ways:

perfume or aftershave

There's no doubt that these cunningly concocted brews can play a great part in sexual allure. Many a man has turned his head when he gets a whiff of the scent worn by a woman who's just walked past him. Too much perfume or aftershave, however, can be overwhelming and a real turn-off.

It's interesting that some of the more expensive scents are actually made from the sexual secretions of certain animals. Whatever their ethics, it's obvious why perfume-makers do this — to create sexual attraction.

perspiration

Since deodorants came into widespread use 40 years ago, humanity has swung heavily towards the idea that the smell of human perspiration is 'not nice'. And it's quite true that on a warm day or after energetic work or exercise, some people who don't use these products can smell dreadful.

It's an undeniable scientific fact, however, that small quantities of male and female perspiration have a pleasantly erotic effect on many members of the opposite sex. If you're a man, male sweat probably smells fairly revolting to you. But many sexually attuned women would say that a hint of it is 'intriguingly masculine'.

Similarly, if you're female then you probably don't care much for the smell of women's armpits.

Yet many men would find just a soupçon of your underarm secretion to be quite a turn-on.

So, one small point of sexual etiquette here: it's obviously the height of rudeness to go round smelling of body odour. But if you want to attract the opposite sex, then there's nothing at all wrong with letting a trace of your feminine/masculine fragrance be detected.

pheromones

The third way in which smell can influence sexual attraction is through natural chemicals called pheromones. We all produce these chemicals from our sex organs, and they have a smell — though we may not be able to detect it at a conscious level. Some are male; some are female.

They're rather like the above-mentioned animal ingredients which perfumers put into scents, though they're much more subtle and harder to detect. Pheromones are very powerful sexual attractants, and it now seems likely that women who produce a lot of pheromones from their sex organs are often able to pull men without the latter knowing why.

The opposite is also true: some men (who may not be particularly attractive visually) seem to attract women just because of the pheromones which are generated by their sexual parts.

Commercial manufacturers have tried to exploit this new knowledge by 'bottling' pheromones in aerosol sprays. The sprays are sold in sex shops and by mail order. Though I have researched this subject for some years, I've been unable to find any convincing evidence that these 'bottled' pheromones — which come from pigs and other animals, not from humans — do really work.

But your own natural pheromones could well attract possible mates. From an etiquette point of view, what should you do about this? Well, social proprieties as well as straightforward medical hygiene demand that you should wash your sex organs at least once a day. But cleaning them to excess (say five or six times a day) will actually wash away your natural pheromones, and probably make you less attractive to potential mates. It can also be bad for you from a health point of view, since it may

encourage infections like thrush — especially if you wash inside the vagina.

Women should also avoid using so-called 'cleansing douches' and 'vaginal deodorants'. In Britain — though not in America — most doctors regard these as potentially harmful, because deodorants may cause a painful sensitivity reaction and douches wash out the natural bacteria which keep the vagina healthy. They will also nullify the attractant effect of your own personal 'come hither system' — your pheromones.

using body language for sexual attraction

There's nothing at all wrong with using body language to attract a potential mate — provided, of course, that you don't overdo it. For a man to stick his crotch out provocatively would be crass. For a woman to stroke between her legs as she's talking to a male (which I've seen some women do — perhaps without being aware of it) is also going a bit far.

On the other hand, giving out negative body language has ruined the prospects for many a potentially good relationship. What do I mean by negative body language? Well, when you meet somebody, and you want it to develop into a relationship, don't do any of the following:

- Drop your head forward as though hiding your face.
- Turn your eyes downwards so that you're not looking at the person.
- Hunch your shoulders.
- Cross your arms across your chest as though protecting yourself.
- Wrap your legs awkwardly around each other as though defending your genitals.

All the above postures are 'barrier indicators', and they suggest to that potential partner that you're putting up defences against him or her, and that you don't want to be approached. (Don't worry, you

Whether a couple become interested in each other depends to some extent on their intimate body smells.

won't be! At least, not unless the other person is unusually persistent or unusually understanding.)

So what is good body behaviour, which will send out signals saying 'I like you' and 'I'm sexy' and 'I think this relationship could develop'?

Well, here are a few hints:

- Keep your head up high.
- Look the person firmly in the eye (this isn't going to be easy if you're shy: in that case, a good trick is to look at a point between their eyebrows).
- Relax your shoulders, keeping them down and slightly back.
- Push your chest forward a little towards the other person — this not only gives them a sense of closeness but (if you're a woman) makes your bust look better.
- Use your hands in gestures that seem to invite the other person's opinion.
- If you can do it without causing offence, and if it seems natural, put your hand on the back of theirs at some stage in the conversation.
- Putting your hand on the person's knee is recommended by some authorities. But remember: this could be deeply offensive in certain circumstances. Don't try it unless you've already had some definite 'come on' signals.
- Open your legs a little, so that your thighs are slightly apart.
- If you feel you must cross your legs, then at all costs, make sure that the upper knee is pointing towards the person you've just met.
- Crossing and uncrossing the legs can be very sexy, particularly in a woman. But if you're not skilled at it, it can look very awkward.
- Moisten your lips while chatting.
- Try to make sure that the other person sees the tip of your tongue as you run it along your lower lip — this is a very strong 'come on' sign, especially when given to a man by a woman.

These are all signals which can be easily read by experienced people. (For instance, last year I was able to detect that a woman was about to be unfaithful to her husband, simply by watching her body lang-uage with another man.) So take care not to give out any of the above signals unless you mean them.

THAT FIRST KISS

There's a time and place for every type of kiss. Kisses between friends or family members are rarely sexually charged, and are usually just a question of kissing the air, making a 'social kiss noise' of some sort while you touch lips. However, a sexual intimacy is usually (but not invariably) implied when you kiss someone on the lips.

Judging when to go for the very first kiss with someone you would like to establish a relationship with — and how far to take that kiss — can be traumatic for anyone who is shy and who probably has desperate fears of rejection. If you are a physical person by nature — in other words, you find it easy to touch others on a friendly basis, and are used to exchanging hugs and so on — you'll probably be surprised that anyone could worry about when and how to kiss a potential lover for the first time. But this causes anxiety in hundreds of people.

The best approach is to do what comes naturally and feels right. If you want to kiss someone, then go ahead. After all, the worst thing that can happen is that the person you are kissing pulls away from you, and the best is that you will receive a kiss back.

If you've only just met someone that you would like to become sexually involved with, you don't have to kiss them passionately on the lips to get your message across. For instance, taking hold of their hand and keeping it in yours for slightly longer than normal will probably convey what you feel. Having said that, most people expect to be kissed goodbye after a first date, so that's most likely to be when you will enjoy the first kiss. Whether it's just a quick peck on the cheek or a more deliberate linger on the lips should be dictated entirely by how you feel at the time and what response you receive.

Kissing inside the other person's upper lip is very intimate and can be extremely erotic.

Note: The question of AIDS and HIV infection is discussed later (see pages 107–8). However, even if a person is infected with HIV, there is such a small amount of the virus present in saliva that there is no danger of HIV infection through kissing, as far as we know at present.

ETIQUETTE of KISSING

If you wear glasses, should you remove them before you kiss? There's no real need — unless the potential partner wears them too, in which case you could get a nasty clash of double glazing. In practice, taking off your specs just before planting that first kiss might well look very awkward. But when you've kissed once or twice, then a slow, deliberate removal of your glasses can be quite effective in suggesting that you really mean business.

When you've got over the preliminaries and are feeling reasonably comfortable with each other, you can then move on to:

- Slower, more lingering kisses.
- Kisses in which you press harder, rubbing lip against lip.
- Damper kisses (these are more sexually charged).
- 'French' or 'deep' kisses, in which one of you puts the tongue into the other person's mouth.

french kisses

There are no rules at all about whether the man or the woman should put their tongue inside the mouth of the person they're kissing. It depends on what gives most pleasure and how the kiss develops. But if you detect any feeling of revulsion or 'pulling back' in your partner, then withdraw your tongue. You may have misjudged his or her enthusiasm for you.

Skilled French kissing is quite an art (see pages 113–4) but don't just confine yourself to what's often

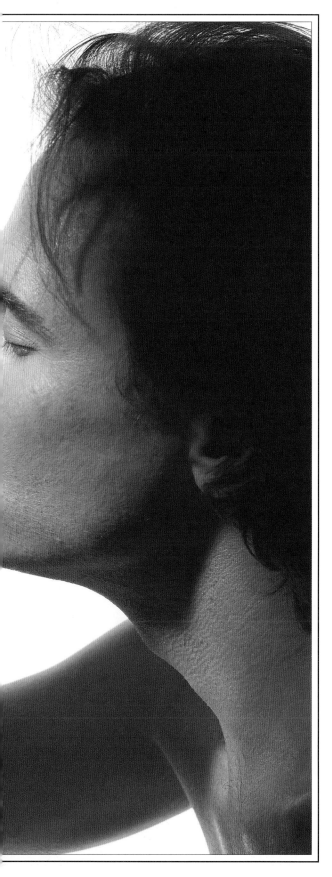

called 'sticking your tongue down the throat'. Try to explore all of your partner's mouth — provided that he or she responds well.

Finally, two important points of etiquette:

- Don't make great slurpy noises when you kiss somebody — particularly the first few times. It sounds ridiculous, especially if others can overhear you.
- Do make sure you don't have bad breath. At the first kiss, more relationships have been ruined by halitosis than by anything else. Cleaning your teeth, using a mouthwash and visiting a dental hygienist regularly will help keep bad breath at bay. If you are worried about whether or not you might have bad breath, ask your best friend.

Incidentally, if you are dining out with a new date and they ask you, for instance, whether or not you are going to have garlic bread or whatever — because if you don't, they won't — it's a useful indication that they have kissing in mind for later on.

should you sleep with
somebody on the
first date?

Well, this is up to you. Statistics show that huge numbers of men and women do — particularly if they're under the influence of alcohol. Another factor which often seems to push people into sex on the first date is simply being on holiday. Frankly, as a doctor I have to say that making love with someone you've met only recently is extremely unwise, whether you're a woman or a man. You probably know very little about the

For some extra erotic sensations when you are enjoying French kissing, try entwining your tongues.

person. He/she could be:

- A psychopath (admittedly unlikely!).
- Married to someone else, though you don't know it (and the someone else could be trouble).
- Carrying HIV (see pages 107–8).
- Carrying some other sexually transmitted disease such as herpes (particularly likely in the case of holiday romance).

So, if you decide to do it, make sure that you use a condom (male or female variety).

going to bed together
for the first time

Whether you do it on the first date or not, there will presumably come a time when you decide to go to bed together. (Of course, it may not be a bed, but on a beach, in the back of a car, or wherever.)

Many first encounters go rather badly, so that one or both of you feels sad or disappointed afterwards. That's particularly likely if one of you was a virgin before the episode: most people have unsatisfactory experiences when they lose their virginity.

The best advice I can give you on etiquette, hygiene, and medical safety is this:

- As implied above, try at all costs not to make love the first time when you're drunk (and your judgement is impaired) though something alcoholic to help you relax will do no harm.
- Do take it very easily this first time and try not to rush things.

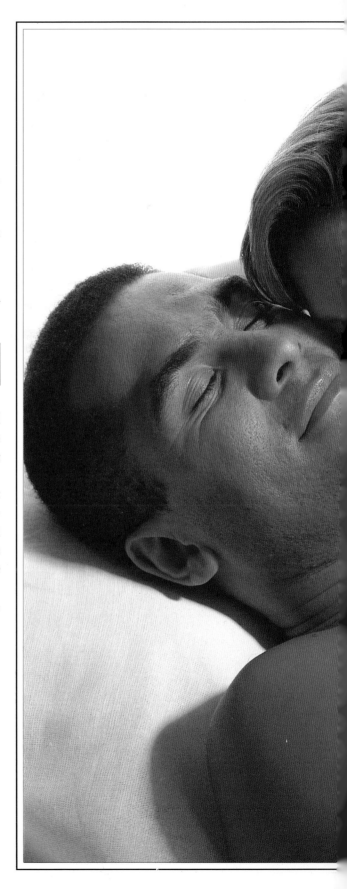

● Going to bed together for the first time requires tenderness, understanding and a sense of humour.

- If one of you is a virgin, try to admit it so that the other person is warned, and can be more gentle and caring than they might perhaps otherwise have been.
- Take plenty of time on your foreplay — make it up to half an hour or more if possible.
- If one of you is nervous, it's best to admit it.
- Be prepared to use a vaginal lubricant — like K-Y Jelly or K-Y Pessaries. When first having intercourse with a new lover, many women are very dry indeed — particularly if there hasn't been much foreplay.
- If you're a woman, bear in mind that your new partner may lose his erection through anxiety. Be prepared to help him regain it, by stroking his penis or giving him oral sex.
- Don't expect too much of each other as far as orgasms are concerned. It usually takes time for sex to be good on both sides, so if you don't expect the Earth to move first time round, you won't be disappointed.
- If you're a woman, you may find it very difficult indeed to come on a 'first night'. Admit this frankly if that's the way you feel — and tell your man that if necessary you're willing to wait till another occasion for an orgasm.
- At all costs, use a condom to protect you against HIV infection. It will also help to prevent unwanted pregnancy, if no other form of contraception is already being used.

raising the question of condoms

One reason why so few couples use condoms is that they're embarrassed about raising the issue. Really, this is madness. From a health point of view, a condom should be seriously considered for any new relationship these days. I am a firm believer in the idea that every man and every woman should carry condoms with them if they think they might finish up in bed with somebody that night.

The male condom (more of the female one in a moment) takes up practically no space, and the famous 'packet of three' can easily be accommodated in a wallet, purse or pocket.

Unfortunately, in the UK there is still a tendency — particularly among the ignorant — to regard a girl who carries condoms in her handbag as a slag. This is wildly irrational, but it's an attitude that still exists.

The situation has been eased by the recent introduction of brands of male condom which don't have a name on the outside of the pack. Instead they have a feminine wrapping, so a woman can carry them with greater confidence that they won't be spotted.

Another encouraging sign is that increasing numbers of women are taking the free condoms which are on offer at all Family Planning Clinics — even if they're already using some other form of contraception.

But assuming that one of you is carrying condoms, you've still got to deal with the moment which so many people find embarrassing: saying that you want to use one. If at all possible, it's probably much easier if you can arrange it so that you have already discussed the topic of AIDS, safer sex and condoms well in advance of the moment when passion takes over and rational thought might be abandoned.

My own belief is that both man and woman should try to agree early on that they will practise safer sex. The phrase 'safer sex' is widely accepted nowadays, and should offend nobody who's got any sense. What it refers to is any type of sexual activity which does not allow semen, vaginal fluids or infected blood to be passed from one person to another, so kissing and masturbation, for instance, are fine.

the female condom

The female condom , also known by the trade name 'Femidom', was introduced to Britain in late 1992. No large-scale research has yet been done to show how effective it is for preventing pregnancy or protecting against sexually transmitted diseases. However, it does offer at least some protection against AIDS. It also gives the woman some degree of autonomy over the question of protection.

Shaped like a small bin-liner, it's made of clear polyurethane, and, like the condom for men, can only be used once. The woman (or her man) slips it into her vagina before intercourse. (One advantage it has over the male condom is that it can be inserted in advance.)

Note: The man must be very careful not to put his penis into the vagina outside the female condom — in other words, slip down the side of it.

PUTTING A CONDOM ON

Many people don't know how to use a condom. This is very risky because if you put in on incorrectly, you may end up with (a) an unwanted pregnancy or (b) an unwanted infection or both. If you haven't worn a condom before, it will help if you practise handling one in private before you need to use it for real.

So what's the correct way to use a condom? Well, a condom (or 'French letter' as it's sometimes called) is just a thin rubber sheath which has to be unrolled onto the erect penis. It's hopeless trying to put it on a non-erect one! You must put it on before intercourse starts.

Having pressed the air out of the teat at the end, put the condom over the tip of the erect penis.

Gently start unrolling it on to the penis, taking care not to tear it with your fingernails or jewellery.

Continue rolling the condom on. If the erection begins to weaken, just give the penis a swift rub!

Finally, roll the condom securely to the very base of the erect penis before entering the vagina.

It is very important not to give in to the understandable temptation to postpone putting on a condom. Many couples let the penis enter the vagina for a while, then withdraw and put on the condom for the final thrusts. This is dangerous, as it exposes you to the risks of both infection and pregnancy — a man can impregnate a woman with seminal fluid before his orgasm.

Here's a step-by-step guide to putting on a condom (always a new one, which hasn't passed its expiry date).

1 Make sure that you don't tear it with your fingernails or jewellery.

2 Take it out of its packet and without unrolling it put it in an easily reachable place.

3 Do not make the all too common mistake of blowing it up to see if there are any holes in the condom because this could weaken it.

4 When you both want to start intercourse — and assuming you have an erection — lie on your back and pick up the condom.

5 Use your finger and thumb to press the air out of the little teat at the end of the condom in order to make room for the semen.

6 Roll it carefully onto your erect penis with your fingers.

7 Now carry on with the lovemaking.

TAKING A CONDOM OFF

Many couples go wrong when they take the condom off — and the result of a mistake can be pregnancy.

The trick is to avoid spillage. If the man just pulls his penis out some time after he's reached his climax, then the sheath may come off, partly or completely. It may even be left inside his lover.

So what you do is this. Soon after he has reached orgasm, and while he's still partially erect, the man should reach down with one hand and hold the condom at the base of the penis with two fingers while he gently withdraws from the vagina.

If you don't do this fairly soon after you come, then there's a danger that sperm will leak out as your penis shrinks inside the condom. Once you're out of the vagina, take the sheath off, tie a knot in it, and dispose of it thoughtfully.

There will now be sperm on your penis and possibly on your fingers — so don't put either anywhere near the woman's vagina till you've had a wash.

problems of
condom technique

People complain of two main drawbacks when using condoms:

- 'My man can't use one.' This probably means that he loses his erection when he tries to put a condom on. The solution is for the woman to put it on very sexily, while rubbing his penis a lot, and saying encouragingly sexy things to distract him. Men appreciate this.
- The condom bursts or slips off. Condoms do sometimes burst, even though they are put through rigorous tests by the manufacturers. It's also quite common for them to come off accidentally, but in fact the condom shouldn't slip off if you follow the step-by-step guide.

If a condom does burst you should consider getting emergency contraception. If treatment is begun within 72 hours after intercourse, the post-coital ('morning after') pill is 96–99 per cent effective in preventing pregnancy. Alternatively, the IUD (coil) can be inserted within five days, with a success rate of nearly 100 per cent. A brief account of contraception can be found on pages 138–9.

SEX and AIDS AWARENESS

Way back in 1984, I forecast that sexually speaking the present decade would be the 'Nervous Nineties', and that's how it turned out to be, although a minority of sexually active people are perhaps still not as nervous or cautious as they should be. In the 'Swinging Sixties' — the so-called permissive decade when people began to be more sexually active — the main fear was of unwanted pregnancy and catching sexually transmitted diseases. These were rarely life-threatening, however, whereas today people should be genuinely frightened of coming into contact with the Human Immunodeficiency Virus (HIV) and contracting AIDS, for which there is no known cure.

WHAT IS AIDS?

The letters 'AIDS' stand for 'Acquired Immune Deficiency Syndrome'. What this means is that the disease attacks your immune system — the defence network which protects your body against infection. Once your immune system has been weakened or destroyed by AIDS, you're easy prey for all sorts of germs.

Virtually all doctors believe that AIDS is caused by HIV. But there are a few scientists — and some journalists — who think that the case isn't proven. Worryingly, there have been a few cases of an AIDS-like illness which is not associated with the presence of HIV in the bloodstream. It's also worth noting that variants of HIV virus have started to emerge.

If you're unlucky enough to catch HIV, the odds are that you will remain well for some years. But you will most probably be infectious, and there is a reasonably high chance that you will pass HIV on to people you have intercourse with (though this isn't inevitable).

After a variable period of years, it's likely that you will develop AIDS — a disorder which is characterized by overwhelming infections, dementia and the appearance of skin tumours (Kaposi's sarcoma). There is no cure as yet, nor is there yet a vaccine against HIV. With such a terrible disease claiming increasing numbers of victims, promiscuity is obviously a very bad idea.

FACTS ABOUT HIV

If the virus gets into someone's bloodstream, it starts to attack the cells which help prevent other diseases from taking hold. There are three main ways that HIV can be transmitted: from mother to unborn child; by drug addicts sharing needles and syringes; and by couples having unprotected penetrative sex (vaginal or, especially, anal).

In an infected person, HIV can be found in all his or her body fluids (including tears), and it can be passed from one person to another through blood, semen and vaginal fluid. This is why there is so much emphasis these days on the importance of using a condom (whether for a man or a woman), and the importance of using it properly (as described above).

HIGH-RISK PARTNERS

If you are about to embark on a new sexual relationship with someone, there's no way you can tell that they might be infected with HIV simply by looking at them. Indeed, the person may not know that they have contracted the virus until years after they became infected. However, some people are statistically more likely to be carrying HIV, so it makes sense not to become involved in a sexual relationship with someone from these groups, at least until you have had a chance to establish the facts about their sexual history, and perhaps until they have had an HIV test. These groups are:

- Users of injectable drugs, like heroin (but not users of oral or smokable drugs like Ecstasy or cannabis).

- Homosexual or bisexual men (lesbians are not a risk).
- Haemophiliacs. (This is because many received infected blood products before tests for HIV were introduced.)
- People who have lived in or visited high-risk areas of the world, and who may therefore have had sex with someone there. These high-risk areas include the whole central belt of Africa, New York, San Franciso, Haiti and Edinburgh, where more than one in 100 younger men are HIV positive. The incidence of HIV in these places is linked to the fact that unprotected sex is very common there (in Africa, in particular) and many injectable-drug users and homosexual men live in the cities.
- People who change their sexual partner frequently.

ETIQUETTE of HIV TESTS

While we were preparing the Good Sex Guide TV series, it emerged that in the Britain of the 'Nervous Nineties', quite a few people think it's OK to ask a new partner to have an HIV test before they agree to sleep with them. At first sight, such a request seems a wise precaution, but it's important to remember:

- It's actually quite difficult — and expensive — to get an HIV test arranged unless you really can produce a good reason for needing one.
- Many people would be deeply offended if a potential mate asked them to have the test.

In practice, there is a strong case for insisting on a pre-sex blood test in certain circumstances:

- If your prospective partner has used injectable drugs.
- If he is a male bisexual.

- If he (or very, very rarely, she) is a haemophiliac.
- If he or she has been living in one of the danger areas of the world listed above.
- If he or she has had numerous sexual partners.

However, do remember that a negative HIV test doesn't rule out the possibility that a person might have recently become infected, but hasn't yet developed any signs of it in his or her blood — the antibodies which prove the HIV virus to be present may not appear in the bloodstream until three months after the infection has been contracted.

WHEN to STOP USING CONDOMS

We found that some people think that when a couple's relationship has got to the stage where they say 'Let's do without condoms from now on,' they should both have an HIV test before abandoning precautions. The practicalities of this can be very difficult, but there may be a case for having a test if one of you is in a high-risk group for HIV. Anyone who does decide to go ahead and have the test should be given careful counselling both before and afterwards.

To date, there are no medical guidelines to help people decide when to stop using the condom. But are there any other points of etiquette about abandoning condoms? Well, the main thing to remember is that doing without them is an important decision which should be taken jointly —so it's not right if the man just doesn't bother to put one on some time, nor tries to pressure his partner against her better judgement.

Whether or not you decide that it's right for you to continue using condoms, the essential point is that you should talk it over carefully with your partner. And if you don't want an unexpected baby, choose another method of contraception (see pages 138–9). Once you have got over the condom issue, you can go back to enjoying sex and learning how to become a more expert lover.

To reduce the chance of contracting the HIV virus, the ideal is to stay in a safe, faithful relationship.

6

Advanced
Sexual
Etiquette

*a*lthough it makes sense to find out about a new sexual partner's background before you make love — and they may want to know about yours as well — a relationship will usually have become well established before either of you trusts the other enough to reveal some things. In particular, it can be difficult talking about your sexual past and you have to decide carefully just how much to reveal.

etiquette of sharing
your sexual history

Your sexual history means the story of your sex life: in other words, how you started, how you lost your virginity, and what you have done in bed with all your previous lovers.

There are two reasons for telling your partners about your past:

■ As already mentioned, in this age of AIDS, it's essential to know who your partner has previously slept with — because this gives you some idea of how great the risks of getting HIV from him or her might be.

- If you're in a long-term, loving relationship, you may want to keep no secrets from the person you love.

Both these arguments were supported by some of the people we spoke to in our research for the Good Sex Guide TV series. But it's important to point out that there are real drawbacks in making a clean breast of your sexual history to your partner:

- Telling all with names could be unfair to your previous partners, who may quite reasonably have assumed that you would keep your relationship with them confidential.
- If your current relationship fails to become permanent, you have definitely given 'hostages to fortune' by passing on all this information about your sexual past to somebody who might one day make the wrong use of it.
- Your partner simply may not be able to cope with hearing about your past. In particular, men often react badly when they find out that the woman they're thinking of settling down with has led an extremely active sex life with a number of other males. An inexperienced man can be horrified to find out that his partner has had more lovers than he has.
- People sometimes react in unexpected ways when they hear about their loved one's past. Some are very turned on by hearing about the exploits of former years. Others may be turned on to start with, but then begin to develop all sorts of insecurities. For instance, men are very prone to say 'Tell me all about his penis — was it bigger than mine?' When told that it was, they may feel sexually inadequate.
- Finally, there's the question of jealousy (a subject which we'll discuss in a moment). There is a very real risk that if you tell your lover about people who've shared your bed in the past, he or she may develop serious jealousy. This is particularly likely to happen if the former lover is known to your present one.

So, you must do what you think best about these disclosures. But go very cautiously — because once you've revealed something, you can't 'un-reveal' it.

ETIQUETTE of JEALOUSY

Following on from this, in any sexual relationship you should, if possible, try to avoid the destructive emotion of jealousy. Severe jealousy, once let loose, can wreck a marriage, or any sexual relationship. It makes people see things totally out of proportion and may rouse them to irrational acts of violence.

Although it's natural to be in some degree jealous of the affections of somebody you love, in a sexual relationship you should try to do two things:

- Stop yourself from getting over-jealous. Don't brood about whether your partner looks at other people in the street or fantasizes about them in bed. Remember it's bad manners to keep asking a partner if he or he fancies somebody, or to keep interrogating them about where they've been every minute of the day.
- Secondly, don't give your partner any reason to be jealous. Again, it is bad manners to tell your partner that you have sexual fantasies about somebody else while making love — except if you're sure that your mate really wants you to divulge this information. You'd better be certain that he or she can cope with it before you open your mouth!

If you find that you or your partner are frequently accusing each other of infidelities, or are acting in a jealous, over-possessive manner, then you should look at your relationship. Are there really good grounds for the jealousy? Or is it perhaps just that your sex life has become somewhat predictable? If sex stops being as good as it once was for you both, then your relationship may be in trouble and you might need to make an effort to improve your love-making.

ETIQUETTE of ADVANCED KISSING

When you establish a sexual relationship with somebody, there are five points to bear in mind about kissing.

1 *kiss as often as you can.*

Many women, and a few men, complain that their partners don't kiss them enough. 'He only wants one thing, and he can't be bothered to kiss me before he does it' is a frequent cry. Such complaints are extremely common after a relationship has been going for a long time and (perhaps) one partner is taking the other one a trifle for granted. Remember: your partner may well regard being kissed as a token of your love; you fail to kiss at your peril!

2 *kiss him/her all over.*

Don't just confine yourself to the lips — go for all the nooks and crannies of the body as well: neck, breasts, nipples, armpits, navel, pubes, wherever. Every secret place in the body is fair game except the anus, which recent medical research has shown to be a definite health hazard for the person doing the kissing. Anal kissing, known as anilingus or 'rimming', usually involves running your tongue around your partner's anus and this activity must now be regarded as unsafe.

3 *don't overwhelm him/her when you kiss him/her on the mouth.*

Some people feel threatened if a great pair of wet lips engulfs the hole they're trying to breathe through! Be guided by what your partner seems to like.

4 *remember that the mouth may be taboo.*

Some women will very happily have intercourse with men, but will not allow their mouth to be

● Awakening your drowsy partner with a kiss at the base of the ear is very romantic and sexy.

kissed while they're doing it! This is an interesting phenomenon which suggests that the woman regards her mouth as a more intimate and special place than her vagina. If you encounter it in your partner, I think you just have to go along with it — and hope that in the fullness of time she will let you kiss her on the lips. But don't push things.

5 *develop the art of French kissing.*
French kissing (deep kissing) was briefly mentioned in the last chapter. It's an art well worth developing, especially when the two of you get used to each other as the relationship becomes more established.

Good variants to try are:

- Put your tongue into the space between his/her teeth and cheeks.
- Raise the tip of your tongue so that it strokes your lover's palate.
- Turn your head so that it's upside-down to your partner's head. Then ease your tongue in so that the top surfaces of the two tongues can stroke each other — a quite unusual sensation.

ETIQUETTE of ORGASM

Inexperienced lovers tend to have orgasms in a most chaotic fashion. When a person is more experienced in bed, he or she should have rather more control of the ability to climax — especially if the couple have been together for some time.

But mistakes will happen, and nobody should be worried if one night, say, the man can't help climaxing too soon — or the woman simply can't reach a climax at all.

Unfortunately, however, there are many men who couldn't care less whether they reach orgasm too soon for their partner's needs. Indeed, they may not care whether she climaxes at all! This is pretty selfish behaviour.

So what constitutes correct behaviour orgasm-wise? Let's look at men and women separately.

men

A man should try to hold out for a reasonable period of time before he has his climax — except on those fairly unusual occasions when the woman says to him, 'Tonight, darling, I want you to go ahead and have me as fast as you like.' (Such things do happen.)

Men should try to remember that women these days want to increase duration of foreplay and intercourse. Some surveys have suggested that the average woman would really prefer over half an hour of intercourse if possible, though few of them get it.

In practice, if you've got good communication with your partner, the best thing is often to ask her after a while if she wants you to go on a bit longer. If she says, 'Yes, I'm loving it,' then try to comply. If she says, 'No, fuck me now,' then you know what to do.

By all means try for simultaneous orgasm if you want to. But, as we've seen earlier in the book, this is quite difficult to achieve. However, try to ensure that your partner gets at least one climax — whether it's before or after yours. Even if you're exhausted after coming, you really owe it to her to try to stay awake and help her if she's not satisfied. Should you help her to multiple orgasms? Certainly, if she wants them; this is the mark of a gentleman!

On the other hand, if one night she says that she really doesn't want to be bothered to climax at all, then you should respect her wishes. There's really very little point in trying to force a woman to come against her will.

women

If you're a woman, then the best thing you can do climax-wise is simply to let your man know what you want, when you want it.

Of course, when you first get into bed, you may not be very sure what you want! But as things build up, whisper in his ear and tell him all about whatever is starting to take your fancy. For instance,

● For an erotic turn-on with a difference, try French kissing upside-down for a change!

as the session progresses an experienced woman who has a good relationship with her lover might well give him a few useful hints and instructions like these:

- 'Would you kiss my clitoris for a while, darling?'
- 'That was wonderful — now could you stroke me inside?'
- 'OK — now I want to feel you in me!'
- 'This is just too good . . .'
- 'I'm going to come any second!'

Most important, do try to let your man know when you're getting near to an orgasm — and when you actually reach it! Many men have considerable difficulty in discerning how excited their partners really are. And if she's not the type who screams the place down when she comes, a man may actually be unable to tell whether a woman's got there or not. That's why some men say embarrassed things like 'Er . . . are you happy yet, darling?' If in doubt, shriek, give a silent scream, or tell him when you come.

Finally, is it OK for you to masturbate to help you reach a climax? Certainly: this is perfectly acceptable these days. Though there are some men who can't cope with the sight of a woman doing this, most of them find it a real turn-on.

ETIQUETTE of ORAL SEX

People tend to have very strong feelings about oral sex. Some are disgusted by it — but a very large number of couples now enjoy oral sex, as our survey shows. But if you really don't like oral sex then you're perfectly entitled to refuse. If you're pressurized into it against your will, it will do nothing for your relationship

Oral sex is an acquired taste but it can certainly give a great deal of pleasure, fun and satisfaction. So it's worth persevering with, even if you're not

● Always try to let your man know when you're about to come by giving some visible or audible sign.

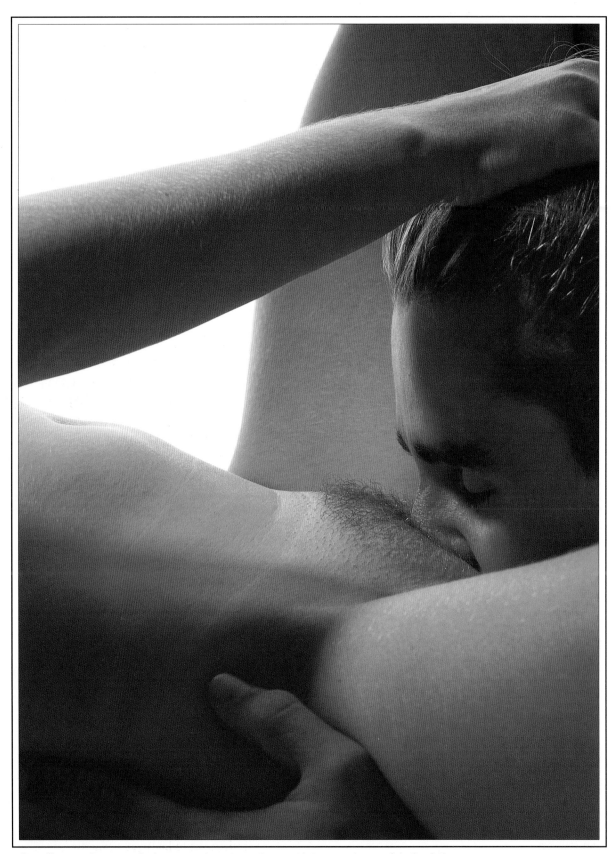

Cunnilingus, when expertly done, can give women the most intense and powerful stimulation.

exactly enthusiastic about it the first time.

Should you be diffident about offering it to somebody, for fear of being repulsed? No, not these days. It's most likely that your partner will be very pleased at the suggestion; and if he or she isn't, then there's no harm done.

One important point of etiquette (and hygiene): you should not perform oral sex if you've got a cold, a sore throat or indeed any kind of infection of the mouth or nose. I say this mainly on aesthetic grounds — after all, who wants their genitals nuzzled by someone with a runny nose? However, there is also a valid medical point here: there are occasions when a mouth infection could be transferred to the sex organs. Most importantly, a cold sore on the lip could give your lover genital herpes.

One final point of etiquette: in my Agony Aunt postbag, I recently received the following rather surprising query from an amorous but somewhat puzzled older reader:

'Dear Doc,
Please advise me. Should I remove my
false teeth before giving oral sex?
Yours sincerely . . .'

This is quite a tricky one — but in view of the increasing number of older people who are enjoying active sex lives these days, it does need to be addressed. My own view is that it would be unromantic to remove a denture before this, or any other, form of sex.

ETIQUETTE of CUNNILINGUS

Cunnilingus is oral sex given by a man to a woman — the term is derived from the Latin word for 'tongue' and the Anglo-Saxon word for 'vulva'.

You needn't be shy about offering your partner cunnilingus: she'll probably be very grateful. And if she's not too keen, she can just politely move your head upwards from her vulva region to, say, her tummy.

Should you actually say that you're going to do it? Well, some men like to enquire 'Shall I go down on you, darling?' but it's a little doubtful if this is strictly necessary. It may be simpler just to get on with it.

However, do not lunge at your partner's vulva, especially if it's the first time you have done this together. Some women are understandably doubtful about a chap suddenly thrusting his mouth between their thighs. So take it easy — a good idea is to approach her vulva very gradually, moving your lips slowly from her breasts, down over her abdomen, and then through her pubic hair.

Once you've started kissing her vulva, do not use your teeth at all — it's an extremely sensitive area. Cunnilingus should be carried out only with the tongue and lips.

One important point for men: please remember that some women become very oversensitive in their clitoris after they've come once or twice. So if your partner suddenly pushes you away from her clitoris, that's probably what's happened. It's almost as if the feeling is too good for her, so do respect her wishes.

Finally, are there any points of etiquette for women to bear in mind while receiving cunnilingus? Yes, and here they are:

■ You must give your man a chance to breathe! Women aren't generally aware that a man can be almost stifled while 'going down' so keep your thighs wide enough apart for him to get some air.

■ Cunnilingus is often very exhausting for a man's tongue muscles, and he may even experience some pain after several minutes' intense stimulation — so don't be offended if he breaks off for little rests from time to time.

■ Do communicate with him (even though your heads are far apart) and let him know if you're getting near a climax.

■ Also, tell him precisely what you want him to do. It's very difficult for the average man who's carrying out cunnilingus to know just exactly where a woman wants him to press.

ETIQUETTE of FELLATIO

Fellatio is oral sex performed by a woman on a man. Again, if you're a woman you needn't be shy about offering it to your partner: most men love it — though even today, a few will reject it because they don't like it or it brings them to orgasm too quickly.

Should you ask him first? You can if you wish; a suitable and generally acceptable phrase is 'Would you like me to go down on you?' But — just as with cunnilingus — it may be simpler to go ahead and do it.

What is acceptable in the course of fellatio? Well, almost anything really — from kissing and tongue-stroking to actual sucking (with the penis in your mouth). But here are a few pointers as to correct behaviour:

- Whatever you do, do not blow. Despite the common expression 'blow job' (meaning fellatio), it is actually very dangerous to blow down a man's penis, since it can cause serious infection.
- Do not bite! This could cause a nasty injury.
- In fact, try to keep your teeth from touching him as far as possible — men do, quite naturally, feel rather threatened by teeth in this area.

Now we come to the two major questions of etiquette that keep on turning up in Agony Aunts' postbags:

(1) Should you let him climax in your mouth?

(2) If he does, should you swallow?

Long articles in women's magazines have been devoted to these two closely linked subjects, but all I can say is that it is a question of your own personal preference.

A man will probably try to persuade you to go all the way — that is, let him climax in your mouth. However, a sizeable number of women simply hate the thought of this. If this applies to you, then don't

be pressurized: just tell him that you're going to take him out shortly before he comes.

Many women will let their partners climax in the mouth, but refuse to swallow the seminal fluid because they find it distasteful. If that's the way you feel about it, then keep a clean hanky or box of tissues by the bed, and dispose of the liquid as soon as you decently can.

Finally, are there any points of etiquette which men should bear in mind during fellatio? Indeed there are:

- Refrain from thrusting too deeply. After all, how would you like having something the length of a banana rammed so far back into your throat that it makes you gag?
- If your lover wants to stop and take a breather, don't be selfish and urge her to go on — she may badly need the break.
- Don't pressurize her to let you reach orgasm in her mouth if she doesn't want to.
- If she does let you come in her mouth, then don't force her to swallow it. How would you like to down something very like raw egg white?

ETIQUETTE of SEXUAL FANTASIES

Most men and women have sexual fantasies — that is, erotic dreams that drift into their minds, particularly while they make love. In one of my large surveys, 60 per cent of married women admitted to fantasizing about sex with another man. However, many people fantasize about their partner, rather than a dream lover, or they have fantasies about an ex-lover, which can cause unnecessary feelings of guilt. It's also quite common for people to dream about making love to someone of their own sex, and then worry about their sexuality when there's absolutely no need to.

- Fellatio is very exciting — but it's important to get questions of etiquette sorted out first!

The majority of people control their fantasies and choose who and what they want to think about, particularly if they are masturbating at the same time. While there's no harm in indulging in the occasional fantasy — indeed it can improve your sex life — how much you can safely tell your lover is a question of good manners.

For instance, if you reveal to your partner during love-making that you are fantasizing about your favourite film star, or whoever you secretly fancy, the revelation could be extremely hurtful. On the other hand, if you don't let him know what you are thinking and you accidentally call out the wrong name during a moment of passion, you are just as likely to cause offence.

Although fantasies are intimate and secret, sharing them with your partner is a good way to make sex more exciting, especially if it has begun to be routine. You should take it in turns to describe what you are imagining or to suggest what fantasy you would like to act out. Different love-making positions can help to make the fantasy come to life. For instance, any position where a man is on top of a woman can help her play out a domination fantasy. Being tied up and forced to have sex is one of the more common fantasy themes among women.

Acting out your fantasies is fine as long as your partner is keen to go along with you. But if one of you likes to do something that distresses the other, you should not pursue it. For instance, some people love dressing up to have sex, but just as many feel utterly ridiculous doing this. It's all a question of finding the right balance with which both of you feel comfortable.

Whatever you do, however, it's important that you should keep the fantasies within your relationship, because if you start to bring others into a fantasy it can have disastrous results. A classic case is when someone suggests (perhaps when slightly drunk) that it would be fun to try three in a bed; it rarely seems such a good idea when they've sobered up afterwards. The 'realization' of fantasies like this often ends up hurting several people and should definitely be avoided.

Above all, you should never reveal your lover's secret fantasies to someone else without permission. To do so would be to betray a huge trust which it would be very difficult to regain. On the other hand, sharing your own fantasies with your lover is one of the most intimate and trusting things you can do and it will help to keep a long-term relationship on course.

Which of the following would you like to do, but feel shy about suggesting to your partner?

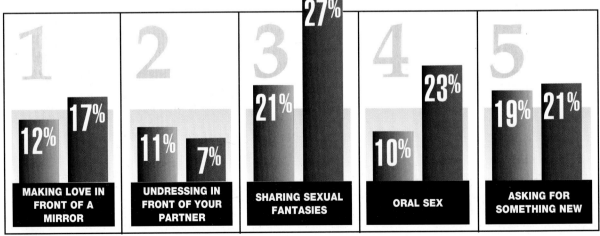

1 MAKING LOVE IN FRONT OF A MIRROR	2 UNDRESSING IN FRONT OF YOUR PARTNER	3 SHARING SEXUAL FANTASIES	4 ORAL SEX	5 ASKING FOR SOMETHING NEW
12% / 17%	11% / 7%	21% / 27%	10% / 23%	19% / 21%

● More than twice as many men (nearly a quarter) than women would like to try oral sex.

Would you like your partner to perform oral sex or would you like to perform it on him/her?

1	2	3	4
18% 43%	5% 3%	59% 41%	11% 4%
MORE OFTEN	LESS OFTEN	THE SAME AMOUNT AS NOW	NEVER

● Nearly 50% of men would like oral sex more often.

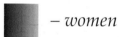 — *women*

 — *men*

Which of the following sexual fantasies, if any, do you have?

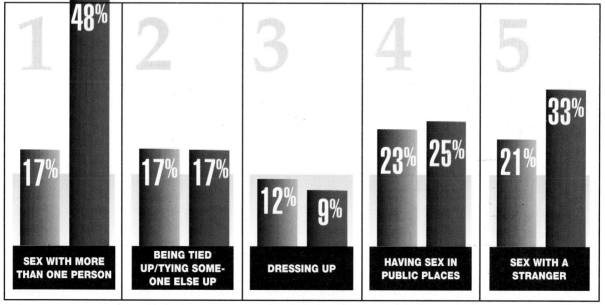

1	2	3	4	5
17% 48%	17% 17%	12% 9%	23% 25%	21% 33%
SEX WITH MORE THAN ONE PERSON	BEING TIED UP/TYING SOME-ONE ELSE UP	DRESSING UP	HAVING SEX IN PUBLIC PLACES	SEX WITH A STRANGER

● Nearly 50% of men fantasize about having sex with more than one person.

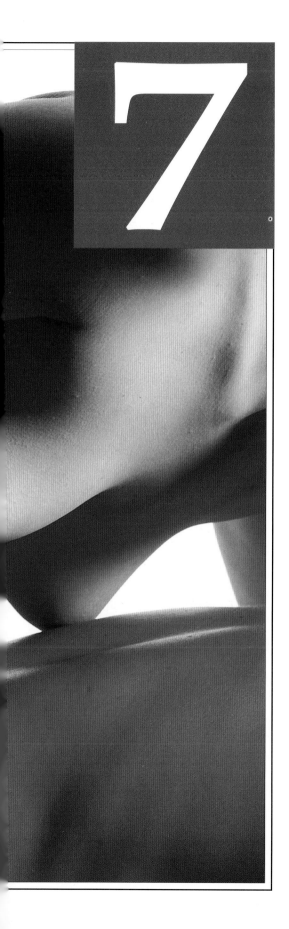

7

Keeping Sex Alive and Fresh

*l*ess than a century ago, sex outside marriage in Western societies was 'not the done thing'. This all changed following the sexual revolution in the 1960s, and it became much more acceptable for couples to have sex before marriage — indeed, it was almost expected that neither of the couple would be a virgin on their wedding night.

This is all changing yet again. These days fewer couples are getting married; instead, many people choose to live together without going through the wedding ceremony. Most important of all, the threat of becoming HIV infected and developing AIDS (see pages 107–8) has meant that individuals have had to reassess their sex lives and behaviour.

LIVING TOGETHER

The ideal situation as far as health is concerned is to live together with somebody, whether you're married to them or not, so that you can restrict your love-making to one partner.

Admittedly, surveys show that huge numbers of people who live together (with or without a wedding) are unfaithful to their partners. However, as a rule such episodes of unfaithfulness are only occasional. Even a relationship with the odd infidelity is far less of a risk than going out and sleeping with three or four new women/men each week.

In a perfect world, the best possible thing would be for a couple to stay with each other for life — without splitting up or ever having any other sex partners. This is, however, a counsel of perfection, and for many people these days a more reasonable aim is serial monogamy — in other words, trying to keep to one partner for as many years as possible, but then moving on to another long-term one when and if the first relationship breaks down.

But there's a big drawback with long-term sexual relationships: sex can get very, very dull if you're not careful.

COPING WITH MONOGAMY

Is it possible to sleep with one person for the rest of your life? Yes, it certainly is — if both of you really work at relieving the monogamy! This means that you need to work hard as a couple in order to keep things as fresh and lively as possible in bed over the years. If you fail to do this, you'll probably find that your sex life resembles sitting down and eating the same meal every night for three or four decades.

Well, how are you going to make things fun for 30 or 40 years or more? The most important thing to bear in mind is romance — at all costs, don't let it seep out of your relationship. Things like candlelit dinners, flowers, little presents, love notes and snatched kisses in dark corners may sound corny — but they are the lifeblood of any sexual relationship that is going to last.

In this chapter, we'll be giving you one or two tips about keeping sex lively and interesting as the years go by. We'll also be looking at what changes you can expect regarding your sexuality as you get older.

sexual activity and how it changes as men age

It's important for men to understand their own sexuality and how it will change through the decades, but it's equally important for women to understand it. If you're a woman in a long-term relationship, you need to have an appreciation of what your partner's body will be capable of (and what it won't be capable of) over the years that you're going to be together. For that reason, I'm addressing this section chiefly to female readers.

Your man's most active sexual period of life was almost certainly well before you met him: when he'd just reached puberty. At that age, boys are bursting with male hormones, and desperate for sexual outlet. At the age of 13 or 14, many boys feel frustrated if they don't have two or three orgasms a day; the average, however, is nearer to three a week.

By the time he's in his late teens, things have calmed down a little — but not very much. Male hormone levels are still very high, and many young men of this age are still obsessed with sex. Most boys are still having around three orgasms a week. Until recent years these mainly occurred through masturbation or through wet dreams, but these days more and more teenage boys have started having sex with girls. The average age when young men lose their virginity has dropped to about 17.

In his twenties, a man's hormone levels start to drop very slightly, and this is reflected in two ways:

1 They get a little less spotty!

2 They become less single-minded about sex — occasionally thinking about other things as well.

Towards the end of their twenties, most men stop behaving promiscuously and try to settle down to marriage, or at least a long-term live-in relationship. There is a further very slight decline in male hormone output when a man is in his thirties, and the results of this include the following:

1 The man's hair often starts to recede a little or to thin on the crown.

2 He is less aggressive than he was in his twenties.

3 His frequency of sexual activity declines by just a small amount.

In his forties, a man's output of hormones drops just a tiny bit more — but it's much less than the fall in hormone output which affects most women in their late forties. So, all that happens is that he probably gets calmer and more sensible; and he probably wants sex a little less than he did in his thirties.

If you — like many women in their forties — are just beginning to get into your sexual stride, then this could be a slightly difficult time. Take the case history of Don and Maria:

CASE HISTORY

Don was 48, and had been very keen on sex in his youth. But he'd let himself get a bit out of shape, and was having a few pints of beer more than he used to. As a result, he really wasn't as active sexually as he'd been only a few years earlier. He was content to make love once a week, then roll over and go to sleep.

In contrast, his wife Maria was a 'slow burner'. She'd led a sheltered early life, and she hadn't been able to enjoy sex or reach orgasm until she was in her late twenties. But now, at 48 (the same age as Don), she was getting to enjoy it more and more. She had bought herself a vibrator, and had discovered the pleasure of multiple orgasm for the very first time.

Predictably, she got frustrated by Don's lack of effort, and she had an affair with a neighbour. Don was very hurt, but it made him wake up his ideas.

He got his act together, lost a few pounds in weight and started working out regularly at a gym and drinking less. More important, he made a point of ensuring that Maria was sexually satisfied several times a week — as well as treating her with more consideration than formerly and being more romantic and loving. Thanks to his prompt action, their marriage was saved.

Men in their fifties have slightly lower hormone levels than those in their forties. But once again, the difference isn't much, and more than 90 per cent of males in this age group are still potent.

Furthermore, a lot of them are actually better lovers than they were 30 or 40 years ago!

Why? Well, it all comes down to a phrase coined by author Frank Harris. He said that when he was a young man, he discovered that, sexually speaking, he had been given a 'wild and inaccurate machine-gun'. It could fire again and again — but it fired all over the place, and he had practically no control over it! But when he reached the age group we're talking about, he discovered that he now had 'a single shot precision rifle'. It only went off once — but he had perfect control of what it did.

This is true for many men in their fifties. They can't have repeated orgasms but they can usually keep going for ages, without any risk of a premature and disappointing climax.

The hormone levels of men in their sixties fall just a little bit more. In fact, around 80 per cent of males in this age group are still potent, and still quite interested in sex. Of course illness may badly affect sexual performance at this age, so there may well be times when you — the female partner — may have to go without intercourse for a while.

Also, many males in their sixties find that although they are still potent, the actual number of erections they have in a day becomes more limited. Often, a man finds that he can reach one erection in a love-making session — but if he then loses it, he may not be able to get it back that night.

If this is the case with your man, you can help him by trying to ensure that he doesn't get the chance to lose that erection. Fortunately, by the time they reach this age many men have learned lots of love play techniques with which they can satisfy their partners in the event of a failure of erection.

What about the over-seventies? Well, in this age group hormone production does at last begin to turn sharply downwards in many cases. And — despite some recent press reports about elderly Members of Parliament having Hormone Replacement Therapy (HRT) — it is very difficult to replace male hormones effectively. As a result of falling hormone output, potency begins to diminish in many men over the age of 70. Again, illness may also often play a part in this.

So, while 70 per cent of men are potent at the age of 70, some researchers have found that less than 50 per cent are potent at 75. However, if a man tries to keep himself fit and active, it is certainly possible for him to remain virile until much later than that, given reasonable luck and an enthusiastic partner. One man is supposed to have sired a baby at the age of 102!

Please bear in mind that even if your life-partner does eventually lose his potency, there is still much that you can do in bed together. Admittedly, many elderly couples are quite glad to be 'finished with all that sex business', but many others really like cuddling up with each other and enjoying a little love play and (with a spot of luck) the occasional orgasm. My researches suggest that a large number of elderly couples have purchased vibrators in recent years.

sexual activity and how it changes as women age

In the same way as women need to know what will happen to their partners as they go through life together, so men need to know what's likely to happen to their women. So, this section is written mainly with men in mind.

Girls reach puberty at about the same age as boys, but as a rule they don't develop the all-consuming interest in sex that most boys have in their early teens. Some start masturbating almost immediately, but others may not do so for many years — and a few never do.

Those who masturbate will probably acquire the ability to reach orgasm while still in their teenage years. Those who don't probably won't. Many women are not orgasmic when they first have intercourse, and it's common for them to have their first orgasm only after they've been having sex

for a couple of years.

In their twenties, most women gradually become much keener on sex, and learn to enjoy it as much as men. By the age of 25, most women are orgasmic, and a substantial minority are multi-orgasmic (which means they're able to reach more than one climax in a session).

It's important for men to understand that the orgasmic ability of a woman usually increases throughout her twenties and thirties — provided that she's got a man who appreciates her, and who keeps sex interesting.

Her ability to reach multiple orgasms is also likely to increase in her twenties and thirties — again, provided that she has a partner who is appreciative and sexually knowledgeable, and who enthusiastically tries to stimulate her.

In sharp contrast to men, women are usually beginning to come to their sexual peak in their forties — especially if they've got contraception sorted out, and don't have to worry about whether sex is going to lead to babies.

In the forties, the proportion of women who are orgasmic is considerably higher —well over 90 per cent — than among younger age groups. Furthermore, the proportion of women who are multi-orgasmic is much higher in the forties than in the twenties or thirties. So, if you're a man with a partner who's over 40, it's vital that you should realize that you've probably got quite a sex bomb on your hands!

Don't give up on sex and romance — otherwise you may lose her.

the menopause

Most women go through the menopause, or 'change of life', towards the end of the forties or in the early fifties. This is when their periods stop. The menopause is caused by a sudden drop in the levels of female hormones — far more sudden than the hormone-drop which occurs in males over a spell of many decades.

Although this book is concentrating on sexual matters, it's important that men should realize that the menopause has many non-sexual implications for your life together. For instance:

- Your partner may well be moody or irritable during this time.
- It's very likely that she will experience distressing 'hot flushes'.
- She may well have very upsetting 'night sweats', which drench her — and you.

So, if the menopause symptoms are bad, she's going to need a good deal of sympathy and understanding. However, quite a few women sail through the menopause with very few problems.

What about sex? Well, surprisingly, the menopause doesn't disrupt women's sexual lives that much. Of course, if your partner has a really bad 'change' with lots of flushes, sweating attacks and perhaps depression, then she's not going to be very interested in sex with you (or anybody) for a while.

However, once a woman has got through her menopausal symptoms, she often finds that this gives her a new lease of life, sexually speaking. A lot of post-menopausal women become interested in sex again, especially as they are now at the peak age for enjoying orgasm. However, men should know that there's quite a high chance that a woman may run into a specific post-menopause sex problem, especially in her fifties.

This problem is called 'post-menopausal vaginitis'. What this means is a fairly sudden drying-up of the previously moist vaginal tissues, because of the rapid fall in female sex hormones. The symptoms are discomfort, and even pain, on intercourse. The essential things for you to know are:

- If you suspect that the disorder is present, don't try to push your penis in hard — this will only make things worse.
- Buy your partner a tube of lubricant, such as K-Y Jelly, from the chemist's, so that you can both apply it liberally (to your penis and her labia and vagina) just before love-making.

If this doesn't work, she needs to see her doctor about some HRT (Hormone Replacement Therapy — see below), often in the form of a cream. This should put things right.

In the fifties and sixties, many women remain very sexually active, and may even take lovers. As she progresses from the sixties to the seventies, your partner may well want to continue to receive sexual satisfaction from you, and it's possible that you may not be able to provide it — at least, not through intercourse alone.

So do be prepared to provide her with alternative means of gratification: love play, masturbation and even stimulation by sex aids. However, all this may not be necessary: there are quite a lot of elderly ladies who have really had quite enough of sex, and are happy to relax into a peaceful orgasm-free old age. Of course, if this is the case and you are still interested in sex, you may need some help from her to achieve satisfaction.

HORMONE REPLACEMENT THERAPY

At the present time, HRT is almost solely used in women — but there are hopes that one day a system may be found for giving men a fillip in later life.

Some people claim that it gives females a sexual boost, but this is a contentious issue. However, there's no doubt that it does help the very common sex problem of post-menopausal vaginal dryness mentioned above. For this particular symptom, it's usually given in the form of a female hormone cream, which, when applied to the vagina, soon restores it to its former state. But it is also possible to treat the symptom with hormone tablets or skin patches, or with implants of hormone under the skin — and there are several different types of HRT available to choose from.

HRT has many benefits, especially in helping to prevent brittle bone disease (osteoporosis), which affects most British women after the age of 60. But it does have its drawbacks and risks, including the necessity to continue having a monthly bleed and some possibility that it may cause breast cancer.

So it is essential that you talk the pros and cons over carefully with a doctor before going on HRT.

● When a woman is pregnant she may find it much more comfortable if the man makes love from behind.

PREGNANCY and SEX

Most women's lives include at least one pregnancy, and it's important to realize how this can affect a long-term relationship.

First, the 'nine months' itself. These days, it's very rare for a doctor to forbid a couple to have intercourse during pregnancy, as was often done in the past.

But things will feel a bit different, especially when the mum-to-be starts producing slightly different-textured secretions, which she will do as pregnancy goes on. Also, as the months progress, the standard love-making positions may become very difficult or even painful for the woman — so it's a good idea to switch to ones which take the weight off her tum (like the Spoons position, see page 85).

Also, during the nine months it is possible that she may suddenly go off sex. This is not common — but when it does happen, the man must be prepared to cope with it. Obviously, he should not try to force her into intercourse she does not want, but should do his best to be sympathetic. If he's very frustrated, he can always relieve his feelings by masturbating.

Loss of interest is however much commoner after the birth of a baby. It happens to thousands of women every year, and is believed to occur partly for psychological reasons, and partly as a result of the hormonal changes caused by childbirth.

If this happens, then the best thing is usually for the couple to go along to a Family Planning Clinic which specializes in sorting out difficulties of this kind by sympathetic counselling. You can get the address of the nearest such clinic from the Family Planning Information Service (071-636 7866).

Finally, men should take note that after childbirth, most women will be very tender 'down below', especially if they've had stitches. So, don't attempt intercourse till your partner says she's ready for it — and certainly not before the post-natal check-up, which is usually done at about the sixth week after childbirth. Even after that, it may be a good idea to use a gentle lubricant for a while.

FITNESS and SEX

Whether you're a man or a woman, you'll do your long-term relationship good if you try to keep yourself fit and healthy. You'll perform better if you're fit — and you'll look better in the bedroom, too. After all, who wants to go to bed with somebody who's getting overweight and out of condition?

Good tips for keeping yourself 'bedroom fit' include the following:

■ Don't smoke.
■ Keep your alcohol intake down to sensible levels.
■ Avoid too much fatty food.
■ Eat plenty of fibre.
■ Keep your weight under control.
■ Take a decent amount of exercise each week.

RELIEVING SEXUAL BOREDOM

At the very beginning of a sexual relationship, when love-making is new and exciting, most couples can't have too much sex. As time goes by, however, it can become mechanical and so routine that it verges on becoming boring. Here are some simple things which might ease the problem if it happens to you.

First of all, is sex something that is confined to the bedroom and only performed at night? If so, try making love at different times of the day and in different places. This might be in another room, or while you're having a shower, for instance. Equally you might find an appropriate place outside — perhaps in the garden or on a secluded beach. If you do choose somewhere fairly public, try to ensure that you aren't going to offend others who might be within earshot.

The other key to keeping a long-term relationship in shape is to try out a different position from time to time. Over the page you will find some positions which are comfortable, fun — and exciting. Why not give them a try when you're in the mood?

trying something new

● **Opposite page:** This comfortable position gives good penetration and unusual pressures on the vagina. The man begins by lying flat on his back on the bed. The woman then kneels astride him, facing away from him. She gently lowers herself on to him, guiding his penis with her hand.

● **Left:** This is rather like the position on the opposite page, but communication between the lovers is easier! Again, the man starts by lying flat on his back. The woman now squats astride him, lowering herself on to his penis, and then gently moves up and down.

● **Below:** This position is particularly good in pregnancy because there is no pressure on the woman's stomach, but it's fine (and fun) at other times too. The woman lies on her back with her legs apart and her knees drawn up. The man curls his thighs round under her bottom and gently enters her.

● **Opposite page:** Positions in which the woman sits on the man usually give deep penetration. Here, the man sits upright on a bed or floor. Facing him, the woman sits on top of him. In most cases, it will be necessary for one of them to guide his penis in by hand.

● **Top:** In this exotic position, commonly known as the 'Narbonne', the woman lies on her back on a bed or other raised platform with her thighs spread wide. Her man stands between her knees and enters her, meanwhile supporting her thighs with his hands.

● **Below left:** One of the 'man sitting' group of positions.It gives deep penetration and leaves the hands relatively free to explore each other's bodies. The man should sit on a firm surface such as a bed or strong table. His partner sits facing him, wrapping her thighs round his loins.

● **Below right:** Sometimes known as the Burgundian position, this one demands a certain athleticism from the woman. It gives deepish penetration, but the inability to kiss during love-making can be a drawback.

Even if this doesn't work wonders, you are more likely to appreciate the positions you usually adopt when you go back to them.

Some couples find it stimulating to look at themselves in a mirror while they are making love. And another popular way to spice up a flagging sex life is to watch an erotic video together or to take sexy photographs of each other.

Treating yourselves to a second honeymoon or having a weekend away from it all can also sometimes help, particularly if you have children and you can leave them behind with someone you trust. Numerous couples go through periods when it's impossible to have good sex because, every time they're just getting into the swing of things, a child walks into the bedroom or climbs into bed with them and interrupts the proceedings.

The most important thing is to let your partner know if you are finding sex a bit dull. That way you can both work on the problem before it gets out of hand.

SEX ISN'T COMPULSORY

If you are completely baffled as to why such a fuss is made about sex, then you're by no means alone. There are plenty of people who have virtually no interest in sex, and there's nothing wrong in that.

Statistics show that there are a number of young married couples who only make love as little as once every couple of months or so — or even not at all. As long as they're both happy with this, then that's fine.

However, problems do arise when a person with little sex drive marries or settles down with someone who is 'raring to go'. This nearly always lead to the build-up of sexual frustrations and in turn can lead to other troubles or even the break-up of the relationship.

Claims have been made for the alleged 'health value' of not having sex, but they have not been substantiated. On the other hand, chastity certainly does protect you against unwanted pregnancy and sexually transmitted diseases.

THE FUTURE OF SEX

There definitely will be one! One thing that the study of medicine teaches you is that throughout the ages, sex has been among the most powerful and irrepressible of all human drives.

So unless the human race is wiped out, sex will go on — probably in much the same way as before, with boy and girl meeting, falling in love and going to bed together.

But with the continuing advance of science, one or two of the following may be developed in the next 20 years or so:

- Drugs to help women who have difficulty reaching orgasm.
- Drugs to help men who are impotent.
- Better vibrator-style devices which will aid the treatment of people with problems in responding.
- Safer contraceptives for both men and women to use.
- A Pill which will be a contraceptive — but which will also prevent breast cancer.
- An 'instant' contraceptive Pill which you can just take on the night you decide to have sex.
- A vaccine against the HIV virus and a cure for AIDS.

The last item is perhaps what humanity needs most during these 'Nervous Nineties'. I hope that every reader of this book will understand that HIV is now a threat to nearly all of us, whatever our sexual orientation.

The virus continues to spread — more slowly than many experts predicted, certainly, but it is already taking a terrible toll of both heterosexual and homosexual lives.

In the future, things are likely to get a lot worse than at present unless people try to lead much less promiscuous love-lives.

This chapter was about keeping sex alive and fresh in a loving and caring relationship — please don't try to do it through promiscuity.

Which of the following would you say are your favourite positions for making love?

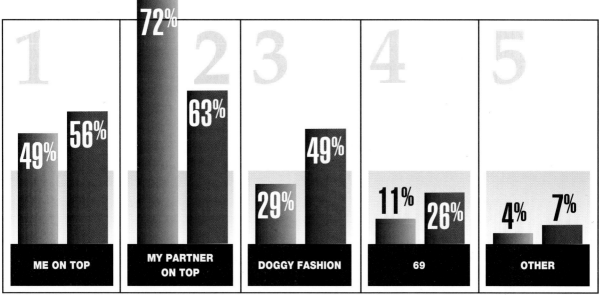

- Surprisingly, 63% of men say that 'woman on top' is a favourite sexual position, whereas less than half of women say this is a preferred position. '69' is favoured by two and a half times as many men as women (figures add up to more than 100% because people were free to choose more than one category).

In the past two years how many sexual partners have you had?

■ — *women*   ■ — *men*

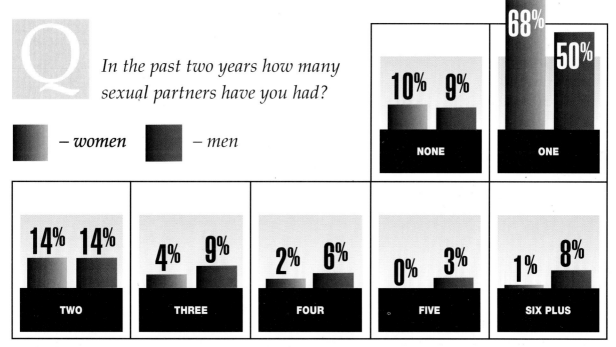

- Half of the men and over two-thirds of women have had one partner only during the last two years. At the other end of the scale, 8% of men but only 1% of women say they have had six or more sexual partners over that time. One percent of both men and women were don't knows!

the various contraceptive methods

I hope you've enjoyed The Good Sex Guide! Now, if you're going to put it all into practice, can I urge you to use some sensible method of contraception? Remember that in a marriage or other long-term and loving relationship, a couple should try to decide jointly on what method they're going to use. Various methods are available at present. However, things change rapidly in the field of contraception, and

METHOD	HOW IT WORKS	PLUS POINTS	MINUS POINTS
The Condom (male)	Rubber sheath on penis 'catches' sperm.	Easy to buy and use.	Can burst. A few people are allergic to some brands.
The Condom (female)	Polyurethane sheath placed in vagina before intercourse.	Like male condom, gives some protection against HIV.	A bit fiddly. Possible for a man to put his penis outside it by mistake.
The Pill	Contains two female hormones which stop the woman ovulating (ie producing eggs).	Helps control heavy/irregular/ painful periods. Reduces chances of some cancers.	Can cause heart attacks or strokes, especially in smokers. May increase risk of some cancers.
The Mini-Pill	Single hormone: thickens womb secretions, making it difficult for sperm to enter womb.	Believed to be safer than the Pill for older women.	Irregular periods common.
The Shot	Hormone injection: stops woman ovulating.	One jab gives woman protection for two months (or more).	Periods may become irregular.
The vaginal ring	Rubber ring releases hormone into vagina: hormone makes it hard for sperm to enter womb.	Kept in for 3 months; does not interrupt love-making.	Sometimes causes period problems. Long-term effects uncertain.
The implant ('the capsule')	Six tiny rubber capsules put under the skin of woman's arm: they release hormone which stops ovulation.	Protection for five years.	Not easy to remove if you don't like it. Irregular periods common. Long-term effects uncertain.

sometimes previously unsuspected side-effects turn up and surprise everybody! So do take a doctor's advice before making up your mind. In Britain, excellent (and free) contraceptive advice is available at Family Planning Clinics, Youth Advisory Clinics and most doctors' surgeries.

My thanks to the Family Planning Association for their help with the preparation of this table.

METHOD	HOW IT WORKS	PLUS POINTS	MINUS POINTS
The IUD (intra-uterine device)	Small plastic and copper object placed in womb; changes womb lining so egg cannot implant itself.	Usually good for long-term protection.	Heavy and sometimes painful periods. Not ideal if you've never had a baby.
The diaphragm (the cap)	Rubber disc, put into vagina before sex to block sperm. Must have spermicide on it.	May help protect against cancer of the cervix.	Very few. Possibly occasional cases of cystitis.
The sponge	Polyurethane sponge, popped into vagina pre-sex as a barrier. Contains spermicide.	Available from any chemist without prescription.	High pregnancy rate.
Vasectomy	Surgeon cuts through tubes which carry sperm from testicles to penis.	Good permanent method (reversal difficult).	Occasional failures. Some worries about long-term cancer risk.
Female sterilization	Surgeon cuts/blocks tubes which carry eggs to womb.	Another good permanent method. Hard to reverse.	Occasional failures occur.
Natural family planning	You confine sex to woman's 'safe period' — judged by temperature charts and changes in her vaginal mucus.	Acceptable to Catholic church.	Only effective in well-motivated, carefully taught couples.

GLOSSARY

ANUS: The opening of the rectum.

ARSE: Anglo-Saxon word meaning 'bottom' or 'anus'.

ASS: American version of arse.

AID: Artificial Insemination (of sperm) from a Donor. Not to be confused with AIDS.

AIDS: Acquired Immune Deficiency Syndrome: (see pages 100, 104, 107–8, 111).

AIH: Artificial Insemination (of sperm) from husband.

BALANITIS: Inflammation of the end of the penis.

BLOW JOB: Slang term for fellatio.
Note: misleading term; do not blow under any circumstances: (See pages 120–1)

CERVIX: 'Neck' (or lowest part) of the womb.

CLITORIS: Small organ located in woman's vulva; important source of pleasure; equivalent of man's penis.

COCK: Penis.

COIL: Type of intra-uterine device (IUD).

COITUS INTERRUPTUS: 'Pulling out' before male climax; very risky and primitive method of birth control.

COME: To reach a climax. As a noun, the fluid produced by a man when he comes.

CONDOM: Sheath worn over penis as contraceptive and also to try to prevent infection. Female condom: sheath worn by woman inside vagina for same purposes.

CRUMPET: In general, a slang term for sexual activity or intercourse (as in 'a spot of crumpet'). As a noun, means the sex organs — much more often female than male. Also used by men to mean 'an attractive woman' or 'a group of attractive women' (eg 'Where's the crumpet tonight?')

CUNNY OR CUNNIE: Archaic version of cunt.

CUNT: Vagina or vulva — or both. Also used pejoratively by vulgar people.

DIAPHRAGM: Disc-shaped contraceptive device, placed in the vagina.

DILDO: Artificial penis, usually hand-held but sometimes strapped on to the woman's partner.

EJACULATION: Squirting of man's sex fluid at climax. Recently, the word has also been used to mean the gush of fluid which some women produce at climax.

ERECTION: Stiffening of an organ (such as the penis, clitoris or nipple) during sexual excitement.

FANNY: In Britain, the vulva or vagina; in America, the buttocks. Do not confuse one with the other.

FELLATIO: Derived from the Latin verb fellare (to suck): sexual stimulation of the penis by the mouth (especially putting the penis in the mouth).

FORESKIN: The prepuce, or 'loose' skin at the end of an uncircumcized man's penis.

FRIG: To masturbate — either oneself or (less commonly) a sexual partner.

GLANS: The soft, velvety cone at the tip of the penis.

HARD-ON: Erection of the penis (not of nipple or clitoris).

HERPES: Sex infection characterized by painful blisters. A closely related form of herpes causes cold sores on the lips.

HOMOSEXUALITY: Attraction to the same sex (male or female): sexual activity with the same sex.

HORMONES: Chemical messengers which travel round the bloodstream.

HYMEN: Thin membrane which partially closes off the lower end of the vagina in virgins.

HYSTERECTOMY: Removal of the womb.

IMPOTENCE: Inability to achieve a good enough erection to make love. Quite often confused with infertility.

INFERTILITY: Partial or complete inability to produce children.

INTRA-UTERINE DEVICE (IUD): Contraceptive device which is placed in the woman's womb by a doctor.

JERK OFF: Masturbate (more usually male than female).

JOHN THOMAS: Penis.

KNOCK UP: (US only) Make pregnant. Not to be confused with British expression meaning to wake in the morning by knocking or ringing.

KNOCKER: Breast.

LABIA: Lips of the vulva (plural: the singular is 'labium').

LIBIDO: Sex drive.

LOOP: Old type of intra-uterine device (IUD).

LOVE PLAY: Sexual caressing or petting.

MASTURBATION: Stimulation of the sex organs with the hand (or sometimes a sex aid). Most commonly means self-masturbation, but can also mean petting your partner.

MENOPAUSE: The time when women's periods stop. Contrary to press reports, there is no 'male menopause'.

NSU: Non-specific urethritis; very common sex infection, characterized by inflammation of the urinary pipe.

ORGASM: Climax; peak of sexual pleasure.

OVULATION: Time (often about two weeks before a period) when a woman releases an ovum, or egg. Often, characterized by a change in vaginal secretions.

PENIS: Male organ; the part of a man's sexual equipment which goes into a woman.

PHALLUS: Penis.

PRICK: Penis.

PROSTATE: Male gland, about the size of a conker, which produces part of a man's sex fluid. Urine pipe passes through it. Often misspelt (and mis-pronounced) 'prostrate'.

PUSSY: Vulva.

QUIM: Vulva or vagina or both.

RHYTHM METHOD: Method of contraception based on attempting to detect the period when it is 'safe' for a woman to have sex.

SCROTUM: Pouch of wrinkled skin round testicles.

SHEATH: Condom.

SLIT: Vulva.

SMEAR TEST: Anti-cancer test in which cells are scraped off the woman's cervix; if done regularly, should provide almost complete protection against cancer of the cervix.

SPERM: One of the hundreds of millions of tiny tadpole-like cells which are found in a man's sex fluid; only one is required to make a woman pregnant.

STERILIZATION: Operation to make a man or woman infertile.

TAMPON: Internal sanitary protection.

TESTICLE: Male sex gland which hangs in scrotum.

THRUSH: Common vaginal infecton caused by 'Candida' or 'Monilia' fungus. Produces irritating 'cottage-cheesy' discharge, in women; men may have redness or soreness of the penis.

TOUCH UP: Masturbate — most commonly another person, but it is possible to touch up oneself.

URETHRA: Urinary pipe.

UROLOGIST: Surgeon specializing in the urinary organs and the male sex organs.

UTERUS: Womb.

VAGINA: Pink female passage which provides a sheath (Latin: vagina) for the penis.

VAS: Tube which carries sperm up from the testicle to the penis.

VASECTOMY: Male sterilization, by cutting through the vas.

VIBRATOR: Mains or battery-powered sexual stimulator.

VULVA: The external female sex organ.

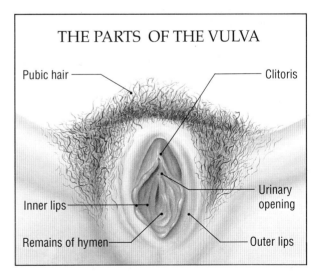

THE PARTS OF THE VULVA

Pubic hair

Clitoris

Inner lips

Urinary opening

Remains of hymen

Outer lips

WANK: Masturbate; or the act of masturbation.

WOMB: Uterus — the hollow organ, about the size and shape of an upside-down pear, in which the foetus develops.

INDEX